# Walking Where the Dog Walks

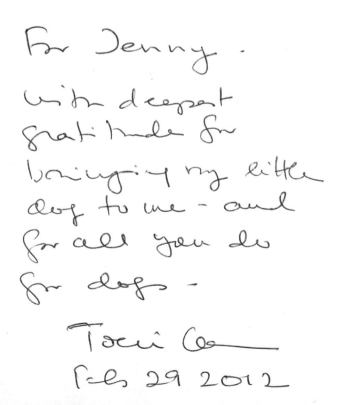

For Jenny.
with deepest
gratitude for
bringing my little
dog to me — and
for all you do
for dogs —

Toni C——
Feb 29 2012

# Walking Where the Dog Walks

*An Interspecies Odyssey in Vietnam, 1968-69*

**Toni Gardner**

Minou Press
Baltimore, MD
2006

Walking Where the Dog Walks:
An Interspecies Odyssey in Vietnam, 1968-69
© Copyright by Toni Gardner
Published by Minou Press
P.O. Box 641, Riderwood, MD 21139-0641
www.tonigardner.com

Photo credits:
All photographs were used with permission from the website of the 47th Infantry Platoon Scout Dog: www.47ipsd.us, where there are many more images of the characters in this story, their fellow soldiers, dogs, and those who came after them.

First Edition

Library of Congress Cataloging-in-Publication Data pending.

ISBN-13: 978-0-9788744-0-7
ISBN-10: 0-97887440-4

Library of Congress control number: 2006933162

Cover: Jim Powrzanas and Rebel, Ashau Valley, 1968.

For my father, Frank L. LaMotte, Jr.,
who read *Kinship with All Life* to me
at an impressionable age,


and for the dogs,
who made it all true

*For my part, I must admit, the romantic and timeless aspects of a man and a dog seeking their sustenance together, relying on each other's special abilities for survival, and accompanied by the ghosts of all such pairs that have hunted together since man and wolf were first allied — that was not lost on me.*

*Lars Eighner*, Travels with Lizbeth

Featured from 47th Infantry Platoon, Scout Dog

Handlers and their Dogs

| | |
|---|---|
| Rusty Allen<br>Saratoga, Texas | Sig KO36 |
| Otis Johnson<br>Columbus, Georgia | Rolf KO86 |
| Chris Mercer<br>San Francisco, California | Dusty (names fictitious) |
| Marvin Pearce<br>Capitola, California | Prince 14M1 |
| Jim Powrzanas<br>Pleasant Grove, Alabama | Pal M596 |
| Larry Proper<br>Meadville, Pennsylvania | Fellow OK88 |

Staff

Stanley Stockdale, Platoon Commander
Atlanta, Georgia

John Carter, Veterinary Technician
Queens, New York

Jonathan Wahl, Platoon Clerk
Roosevelt, New York

# Contents

# Preface

During the Vietnam war, as in all wars, dogs were used to support troops in various ways—as sentries, trackers, tunnel detectors, and mascots. But scout dogs, mostly German shepherds, performed the most daring work. These were lively, boisterous dogs in civilian life who found their destinies fulfilled leading infantry platoons on missions through the jungles, rice paddies, grassy lowlands, and burning beaches of Vietnam.

The dogs did not walk alone. At the end of the leash they were accompanied by trained handlers, reluctant soldiers for the most part, the oldest barely out of their teens. For them, "volunteering" to become scout dog handlers had meant a few extra months of training in the States. They hoped the war would end in that time. They were not thinking about dogs when they signed up to be handlers.

But the war did not end, and together they went to Vietnam and into a shared experience that would change everything.

*Walking Where the Dog Walks: An Interspecies Odyssey in Vietnam, 1968-69* is the story of a group of men who found themselves in the U.S. Army, who trained together at Fort Benning, Georgia, and who, individually, found dogs in the kennels there that would make indelible impressions on their lives. It is the story of their year together, through the training they thought would prepare them for the war, and through the long months when they lived, and when some died, in that war.

For most dog handlers in the Vietnam era, training at

Fort Benning with one dog was followed by a voyage to Vietnam and the assignment of a new one. But for the handlers of the 47th Infantry Platoon Scout Dog, the dogs they trained with were the very ones they brought over. The dog-man teams were bonded, in sync, before the main event began. They were new together, and, as close friends, would face their most terrifying and visceral months at war together.

Many of the men in this particular unit had met in basic training. They'd been through basic, advanced, and, for some, parachute jump training. An unusually large number were officer school dropouts. It was a strong unit, built with confidence, trust, and fellowship.

The fellowship that existed among the men also came to life between the men and their dogs. This was not the case for every dog-man team, and this book does not falsely sentimentalize or gloss over the reality that some teams worked and some did not. Some dogs had great abilities, while others could not manage the crushing pressures of the job. Some men worked well with their dogs, but saw them only as a tool, no more valuable than their M-16s. Some could not reach inside their dog to understand that animal. But others could, and did. This relationship changed their war experience and transformed their inner lives as well.

This is the story of six men who developed, in their own ways, an intuitive communication with their dogs, and whose consciousness was expanded when they learned to open their minds to another species. Because it is a war story, it is about loneliness, fear, betrayal, and death. It is about being an American boy who suddenly finds himself halfway around the world in a strange place where nothing is as expected, where nothing unfolds according to plan, where you are hot and filthy, where people are trying to kill you. Unlike other soldiers, these had a dog to consider through all of it.

The dogs were friends who kept them company and bolstered their confidence. They were specialized workers who gave them status and protection. Together they saved lives of whole platoons and companies. But they were also called on to walk point, the most dangerous position in the patrol, and the dogs also hindered the men's ability to defend themselves in firefights. And sometimes the dogs went crazy and put everyone in danger. Whatever happened, though, the men and dogs acted as one, literally and emotionally, changing the very fiber of their identities.

The book follows the development of these relationships, the gradual unfolding of friendships that took place over a year—as the men and dogs mature from green recruits to bewildered and then seasoned soldiers.

But the central character in this story is not necessarily any individual man or dog. It is the relationship between man and dog, the brotherhood that was born out of their connection, that grew, faced conflict, strengthened and deepened, and though separated by distance, death, and time, still lives inside those men. It is about the difference a dog can make while living through war. It is about how a dog can change a person.

What can a story about a boy and his dog tell us? It can talk about friendship, integrity, loyalty, endurance, and courage. It can speak of tenderness and humor, of fear, of a mutual refuge, and of private communication between two who are a species apart, but joined together in an indefinable, higher place. The story of this singular relationship points the way for us to experience in our own lives the extraordinary richness possible in the kinship between humans and dogs.

# Walking Where the Dog Walks

They called because of the mines. They were in the field--moving out along this trail for three days, seeing what was there, just now entering into some brushy area on the side where there were some rice paddies and who knew what else or who else they might find.

They were part of operation Nevada Eagle, begun in May of 1968, and now, six months later, still going. They were walking out to find where the North Vietnamese Army was moving into the south and where they were hiding. They would find them, and their Viet Cong helpers, and engage them in combat when they could. It was a Cordon and Search operation, circle around and then close in, and it also entailed "rice destruction," the attempt to cripple the enemy by destroying his weapons and supplies.

As farmers curved over the brown-green water, pulling out the slender strands of grasses, all appeared benign, timeless, orderly. But here nothing was ever completely routine or predictable. You could never truly relax. You never knew which kind of surprise you would get or where it would come from, and something nearly always waited for you. There were variables you could half-expect and that you developed an unconscious watch for. Sniper in a tree up ahead. VC under the brush poised for small arms strike-and-vanish act. Snakes— three hundred poisonous varieties here, including one that glided out of trees. Leeches dropping out of trees and into your shirt, sneaking into your armpits or up your legs. Well of water that might be poisoned. Or it could be the surprise of a patch of trail, smooth or sandy as the rest, that covered a pit of sharpened sticks--sticks carved with barbs, coated with human waste, and placed so that when you fell in you'd be impaled by them, but if you pulled out you'd be grabbed again. Then you wouldn't necessarily die, but more likely your body would rot away, in parts, with gangrenous infection. The other men wouldn't just lose you in an instant, but could also be wounded by proxy, knowing and even watching your agony and dismemberment. Those images could last longer and work into the psyche and maybe make you that much less interested in completing your mission, which already might not make that much sense to you.

Mines and booby traps worked on the same principle. They might be Chinese- or American-made (and VC-foraged) bombs attached to trip wires. These could also be command-detonated: NVA or VC would wait for you, watch you when you couldn't see them, and detonate them right on you. This was at the height of America's involvement in the war, when mines and booby traps accounted for nearly one quarter of

American combat deaths. Overall, these devices caused seventeen percent of American casualties in Vietnam (and eleven percent of deaths) versus World War II's two percent of casualties caused by mines and booby traps.

The explosives ranged in size from full-sized Claymore mines or bombs all the way down to "toe poppers," fashioned from scrounged U.S. rations cans — garbage that was supposed to have been buried, and might have been. Sometimes the small cans contained extras, nails, scrap metal from weapons or other machines including helicopters, wire, can openers, used batteries, ball bearings, glass, and anything else that would tear flesh, with explosive added. Or it could be a grenade inside a small can, with the pin pulled out but the safety lever held in by the can, then released by someone stepping on it or on a wire across the trail. Or the grenade might have been packed into mud. When the mud dried, the pin was removed, so that when someone walking along a trail accidentally kicked the piece of mud, it exploded. The North Vietnamese, and especially the Viet Cong, didn't have the resources we had, so they learned how to find bits and pieces that were ours, seemed meaningless to us, and figured out how to painstakingly refashion them, bit by tiny bit, into things they could use against us. Some say ninety percent of these devices were made with our own cast-off supplies. And among those things were these mines.

This unit was working northeast of Hue, along the coast in I Corps, one of the four Corps Tactical Zones that the U.S. military had decided comprised South Vietnam for purposes of planning and strategy. And now it found itself bound in by mines, held prisoner by earth-covered or brush-concealed bundles of shredded metal and slivered glass and explosives that could decimate a foot, a leg, an abdomen--for they were often aimed for the U.S.-height groin—and annihilate a life.

They had gone out there and they had found themselves in the middle of a spider's web of explosives, unable to go forward or even to retreat. Already two men were down and the lieutenant wouldn't risk another.

So they called for a dog team.

They waited for the helicopter that roared in, loaded the wounded, and lifted out, quickly so it wouldn't become a target. And they waited, not saying much, if anything, for the dog and the man.

Back at Landing Zone Sally, Larry Proper was at the top of the board. It had been less than a week since his last mission, but the dog teams of the 47th Infantry Platoon Scout Dog were being called out a lot these days, and when your name rotated to the top of the board, unless someone called in with a special request, you went. Or the platoon lieutenant, Stan Stockdale, might tag you for a mission because you and your dog were especially good at something--high altitude or bad weather or brushy trails or personnel or bunkers or mines. There were no absolute systems here either.

Their tour lasted a year, and during that stay, they would be called on by a variety of Army units, usually those from the Second Brigade of the 101st Airborne Division. They would lead patrols through the rice fields, the jungles, the lowlands, and the rocky mountainous trails that together made up the terrain from Hue to the Demilitarized Zone in I Corps, the northernmost section of South Vietnam. Dog-man teams would be dropped out of helicopters and into these areas to find the things that had eluded human detection, but that the dogs would target and identify with their superior sensory abilities. By conservative estimates, each dog would save an average of ten American lives. They would foil enemy ambushes, pinpoint snipers in trees, reveal mines and traps, and prevent friendly fire, among other accomplishments. And they would not work without some failures as well.

Each handler in this platoon had trained with one dog, and unlike most other military dog platoons in this war, that animal would go over to Vietnam with him, become first his partner, and then ultimately his second self, for the duration for the tour.

The handler alone knew how to interpret the dog's silent language--the tipped ear, the raised haunches, the frozen stare--and the handler would know not only that there was danger, but precisely what form that danger took. The man would serve as the medium through which the dog could communicate his knowledge, because the dog would know well before the man where things were hidden--where there were people, weapons and other supplies, booby traps and mines, secret tunnels, camps, villages, and also snakes, monkeys, or water buffalo. They had been thoroughly trained to search and find, but in the scrubby pine forests and salt marshes of Georgia, not the suffocating heat and frightening, bizarre geography of I Corps, and not with the same stakes. The dogs had been trained on a positive system of reward, not punishment.

Jonathan Wahl, the unit clerk, took the call, a simple request, no details provided since none had been given-- to prevent interception by the enemy. In the fall of 1968 the Tet counter-offensive was still underway, and while some areas saw less action that year, I Corps did a brisk business.

Proper packed his gear--three days worth of everything: ammunition, rations, canteens, socks; and three days of gear for Fellow too: cans of dog food, bags of dry dog food, canteens for the dog, doubling the load of water. With water-purifying tablets, heat tablets, insect repellent, towel, poncho, poncho liner, knife, .45 revolver, and M-16 automatic rifle, the rucksack weighed a good seventy pounds.

They had been review-training earlier in the day, and now Fellow was resting under Proper's cot. It was, or at least it seemed somehow, not exactly cool but just less hot in there than at his stakeout in the kennel area. The thick, sickening heat held little mercy for a German shepherd, this one solid black except for the brown exclamation-point eyebrows that Proper thought might, in the dark, look like extra eyes to frighten anyone they might encounter at night. The heat didn't do much for Proper either, who pushed on his heavy, clumsy helmet.

Fellow was aware. He lifted those exclamation points and jumped up ready and excited, with the naive, joyful anticipation of preparing for a favorite game. Fellow's intelligence easily translated all this activity into the knowledge that he was on his way to a mission; his innocence allowed him to expect the best, to bend himself back and forth in happiness, unfrightened at the prospect of heading out on an adventure with his human partner, where he would be challenged to use his learned skills, his instincts, and his naturally endowed senses. It was time for the Big Game, and he was always ready.

Dogs remember what happened last. People who live with dogs witness how a dog reacts to going to the veterinarian, or to your leaving the house without them. If these dogs had been afraid of what would happen on missions, where they'd experienced plenty of unpleasant moments, they'd have tried to avoid going. They'd have hung back, whined, or hidden. But these weren't that sort of dog. As a whole these dogs exuded confidence, enthusiasm, and optimism, even though they remembered what had happened the last time they'd been on that helicopter ride. Or maybe they were just thinking about the ride, up in the only cool air, where they could lose themselves in the wind, soaring up and out with their human wrapped around them.

Fellow was now highly trained, solid and true, ready for these adventures, a willing soldier. Scout dogs had to be bolder than the average dog, but smart, had to be able to listen to the voice of his handler, had to be able to bond with a person. Though some had been gun shy in the early stages of training, they'd overcome it (or been dismissed). Others had been too fierce, too aggressive, and had become sentry dogs instead, if workable. Scout dogs weren't warriors, because they did no actual fighting. They weren't trained to attack anyone, as the sentry dogs were. When they found the people or traps, they were sent to the rear of the platoon because they were needed to find the enemy and his paraphernalia and should be protected from the action so they could survive to find again. Their purpose was to save, not take, lives.

But they had minds of their own that didn't necessarily shut down because, in the Army's mind, their assignment had been completed. They were known to have gone after NVA or VC soldiers firing directly at them, and to have lost their lives that way.

When the dogs came up against the Vietnamese, the animals exhibited the body postures and facial positions that are generally accepted to indicate an aggressive-threatened posture with readiness to attack — the stiffened legs, raised back hairs, upward thrusted head and tail, forward ears, teeth-revealing snarl, locked eyes. Everything that worked toward the trust between the handler and his dog was turned inside out when the dog confronted the Vietnamese.

This was true even with the South Vietnamese at first, when the dogs entered the scene on the advice of the Military Assistance Advisory Group, Vietnam, early in the sixties. Sergeant Jesse Mendez, head of dog training at Fort Benning, and other instructors, came over in 1962 to get the training and care of the dogs straightened out. Was it the looks or the speech--its tone, inflections, or content--of a race of people different from their handlers? Or was it simply that the Vietnamese were in general afraid of the dogs, perhaps causing them to exercise the quick, jerky retreat movements that would further stimulate the dogs' aggression? Did the dogs detect a wall of mutual distrust between their handlers and the Vietnamese, even the South Vietnamese?

It makes sense to deduce that the dog was able to comprehend the threat of the enemy as an extension of their handler's enduring emotional state of fear and aggression toward the North Vietnamese and Viet Cong while hiding from him or while hunting him. And maybe they had sensed distrust between Americans and their South Vietnamese allies too. Sometimes they suspected them when their handlers didn't: one dog persistently attacked his platoon's "Kit Carson" (South

Vietnamese) scout while on a mission. The scout was eventually found to be Viet Cong, his rucksack loaded with a Chinese-made grenade intended for this patrol. He hadn't fooled the dog for an instant.

Though the dogs weren't intended to be used against personnel, U.S. soldiers quickly recognized their enormous potential as a perceived threat to a prisoner of war. Their mere presence at an interrogation became an effective force for eliciting information from captured North Vietnamese or Viet Cong. The dogs, bold strapping German shepherds, were the prisoners' equals in size and weight.

While the dogs were being trained a world away at Fort Benning in Georgia, the quarry they were trained to find consisted of American men. They were taught to find, that's all, people or mines or tunnels or things that just didn't belong there in the dirt or the tree or the brush. And sometimes, later when they were in Vietnam, for a minute they became regular dogs again, forgot themselves and ran down a water buffalo, or even a village cat, instead.

They accepted the infantry platoon members with whom they and their handlers worked their missions, almost always a new set of people each time out, maybe because their handler told them to or maybe they could read the signs well enough. They understood the body language and voice intonations of their handler. As the Americans in the unit greeted one another, maybe not joyfully but at least peacefully, the dogs could recognize the mutual acceptance. A dog's mind won't hold the notion of a geopolitical war, but dogs are all about pack integrity. If a handler brought his dog into this new pack, it was okay with the dog. He looked up to his handler and respected his intentions. But the dog also protected his handler, and some did that with teeth if infantrymen got too close, in the dog's mind, to his handler.

An unneutered male dog, which is what most of the canine scouts were, is ready to take on a conflict, and these lionhearted dogs had been trained to see the handlers' conflicts as their own. They wouldn't have been afraid to face them, including a search that could end in explosion or gunfire and pain. Wounded dogs, if they could recover, were sent back to work as soon as they were fit. Many of them knew about the pain, but the dog loved his work. Part of that was the search-game with the handler, and part of it was also the opportunity to protect.

The dogs were aware their handlers' fear. They know, and their own senses sharpen up, focus in, prepare to defend the handler, who is no longer an Other but has become an Us. That empathic acceptance usually seems easier for dogs to manage than humans, but in this place at this time the most attuned handlers got it, too. The genetics of pack or family or community mentality are etched into our own human cell structure as well as the dogs', and was now called on.

The dog would lead his handler at the head of the platoon, as they moved together into the elements. The working harness now replaced his choke collar and lead. That confirmed everything. This was about being together and serious now, in focus, wary, and searching.

Waiting in the heat at the landing zone, the dog Fellow stood up seconds before Proper could hear the low percussion of the approaching Huey. The helicopter soared in, flattening Fellow's black coat as he lifted his nose to feel the wind of the blades; then Proper heaved the scrambling, eager dog into the open helicopter and jumped in after him. He settled them both down, hanging on to the leash and his M-16, while they swooped out again, over the red dirt of the landing strip.

The men were strung out along the trail, or the series of trails, through the field of high grasses edged by spare saplings. They were frozen into their positions. It was hot and sunny, and there was no wind or even breeze until the helicopter bobbed in at the rear, where it was safest, and was out again, and lifted away its breath of air.

Proper faced the tangle of brush and the grasses, razor-edged and six feet high in places. He could barely see over it. It was green, but not soothing, an acid green, and thick enough to conceal an arsenal of traps.

The dog-man team was greeted with respect. In his typically understated fashion, Proper nodded, and noted only that the frightened men seemed anxious to get out of the situation and that he and Fellow needed to get right to it.

Scout dog teams were expected to handle a variety of situations, and as they walked together at the head of a platoon, sometimes with another soldier walking shotgun nearby to cover them, individual dogs developed their own methods of communicating their knowledge to their handlers, sometimes in an idiosyncratic fashion.

Otis Johnson's dog Rolf was a veritable actor, with an impressive repertoire of signals that became part of the language of their shared communication. If a sniper was in a tree, Rolf would squat down and fold his ears back. If the quarry was on a mountainside ahead, he would freeze and stare and refuse to move. Johnson would

11

know right away if there were livestock in the area: Rolf would sit up and put his front legs in the air. For detecting a mine, he would freeze and point his head down directly at the mine location.

Jesse Mendez, the trainer and sergeant from the Ft. Benning dog school, would dismiss such descriptions. Dogs were trained to stand at a silent freeze with ears up and forward for a personnel alert, and to sit for a booby trap or mine alert. This was the school method. But handlers working in the field knew otherwise.

Every dog had his own signs, usually slight variations from the standard alert. As Rusty Allen would later explain to new handlers, "That's why it is so important to have that close relationship with your dog, to work and train together constantly even when you aren't out in the field. Some of the alerts are really subtle, and if you aren't close with your dog, you'll miss it, and that could be it."

Fellow's personnel response was a quick action--ears up, and eyes and ears in line with the enemy. A glance away, and Proper could miss the signal; he could walk straight into an ambush. For trip wires, Fellow would freeze in his tracks. Since these fine, taut wires were nearly invisible to the human eye, the halt would cue Proper to kneel and carefully search the air in front of him until he saw it. Fellow would already have heard the air moving over the wire. For punji pits and mines, Fellow simply walked purposefully around them.

And now the training mantra rang in Proper's head, shutting out all other thoughts, *Walk where the dog walks. I am just walking where he walks*. By this he meant each step. Proper knew his dog completely, as the dog also knew him.

Training had been one thing. There they'd mastered the mechanics together and become a friendly team, buddies. But once they'd arrived in-country, the bar had been raised, and suddenly there the mutual trust expanded into a palpable energy. Trust took on a surprising magnificence: the closeness they developed with their dogs affected the men; it elevated them, comforted and strengthened them. They were unto themselves, their own unit of two, always together in a place where a person could be terrifyingly alone.

From the rear, Proper and Fellow advanced together with the energy that existed between them, a confluence of skill and intelligence, energy, affection, and trust. They paced each step, deliberately and slowly, along the trail--Proper ducking the brush but not looking at it, only watching his dog; Fellow in a hyperfocus, all distractions tuned out, knowing this job must be perfectly executed, and knowing why.

Did he do it for survival, for the game, or to please Proper? Looking at it another way, was he absorbing all he'd been taught, targeting his mind, releasing the power of his natural senses--smell, hearing, sight, and perhaps another or so that we've not yet been able to measure-- did he knit all these parts of himself together and transcend being a dog to become a dog-man force, attuned to itself and to all that surrounded it, so the work of the mission was not for this person or that game but altogether the purpose of existence?

If you can believe that people give off an energy--by scent or pheromone--that can be detected by animals, and that fear is probably the easiest to detect, you can believe that the dog absorbed the fear-electricity that surrounded each man. But he was undeterred by it or maybe energized by it, his senses now heightened even beyond their already exquisite powers.

With his nose to the trail, he moved with slow steps, unhurried, completely in and of the moment and not projecting, calling on his intellect, his instinct, his senses, his training, his bond to Proper. And sometimes the steps would ease into a lower gear, his legs stiffening ever so slightly, and the shoulders tightening as he lowered his body; then he would loosen the tenseness and move on, more smoothly now, past or around a something that seemed wrong to him.

One by one he reached and then moved past the men, and each time Proper signaled them to follow, reminding them, "Walk where the dog walks. Exactly in his steps and in my steps." And each man in his turn gave over his trust to the dog and the man, seeing that Proper and the dog were moving in perfect unison and in safety. One by one Proper passed them, each step in the step of the dog. One by one they fell in behind him, also in the same steps, until at last the relative safety of their destination of the rice fields appeared, not three hundred feet away. Oblivious to the heat, and with those achingly deliberate steps, the sometimes poised foot and sometimes walking off the trail and into the stinging brush, all of them, from the rear to the front, were led out of the area without a single casualty.

---

Notes

Mines: Ebert, pp. 189-95; Lemish, 269 (nts. 19 and 32); O'Brien, *If I Die in a Combat Zone*, pp. 125-29.

Activity in I Corps: Spector.

What they carried: Sykes, "Another Mission," *Dogman*, vol. 1, no. 5 (Dec. 95), p. 1.

Hatred/fear of Vietnamese: described by numerous sources; Kit Carson story from 47th guest book, 7/30/99, Craig Latham, 34th PID, Airborne.

Body postures: Fogle, p. 64; others.

Jesse Mendez, phone conversation re Rolf/Otis Aug. 6, 1999.

An article from *Danger Forward*, the magazine of the Big Red One (1st Division), *Vietnam*, vol. 3, no. 2, June 1969, noted the variety of alerts that existed, including a dog, Major, who "has the strange habit of crossing his ears on an alert, while Eric puts on an acrobatic act by walking on his hind legs."

Dog-human empathy: Arluke and Sanders, pp. 61-81.

# Gone to Soldiers

On May 27, 1968, two C-141 Starlifter cargo planes landed at Tan Son Nhut Airbase near Saigon, Republic of Vietnam, carrying the freshly formed 47th Infantry Platoon Scout Dog, a United States Army unit that consisted of a commanding officer, sergeant in charge, clerk, veterinary technician, and four squads of six men each. As a new unit, the 47th came equipped with four two-and-a-half-ton trucks, one jeep, six medium tents, two M-60 machine guns, a grenade launcher, and enough .45-caliber pistols for each man. They had also managed to pick up and include among the provisions a couple of used refrigerators. In addition to the men and the equipment, on board were twenty-eight dogs, now rousing themselves, heavy from a sedated sleep, four of which would be assigned to other units needing replacements.

Many in the unit had dropped out of, or been dropped from, officer candidate schools, and all of the handlers' level of both training and education significantly exceeded that of the average infantryman going to Vietnam. With the exception of one man, Marvin Pearce, this was the last place on earth any of them wanted to be. Throughout their training, each man had entertained the notion that he'd never actually go to this strange place, and an identity as a dog handler, a Dog Man, was at best only loosely formed. Interspecies completeness was the furthest thing from their minds.

These young draftees and former officer candidates had checked in for scout dog training at Fort Benning, Georgia, early in February of 1968. They had no notion then of the conditions in which they would come to live and the interdependence they would achieve with an animal. Though officially "volunteers" for the twelve-week training, these men were not there because of a love of dogs or an eagerness to work with animals. They hadn't wanted to go to Vietnam, or be in the military at all. But the draft was swelling, and was bringing in an all-time high of thirty thousand men a month by August of 1967, and they were pulled along with it.

By this time even the conditions for college deferments from the draft were tightening. Rules fluctuated. If you slacked off, your grades might drop, and suddenly you're eligible. Such was the fate of Stanley Stockdale, at Emory University in Atlanta, Georgia, who would become the unit's commanding officer.

Stockdale's first assignment would be completing the selection of men for the unit. Some, high achievers like Otis Johnson and Jim Powrzanas, had already been put on his list, plucked from regular training programs; the remainder would have to be drawn from the First Casual Company, a conglomeration of washouts from other training programs. Experience with dogs did not figure into any of the selections.

Since the men could have turned down the assignment, all who accepted did want to participate, but their reasons had nothing to do with dogs. It was simply that dog training would give them three more months in the States, and when they did go to Vietnam, as they feared was inevitable, they would spend the bulk of their time in base camp between short missions, so would not always be out in the field. They might be less vulnerable. The dog program bought them some time, and if they'd been offered another option that kept them out of Vietnam a day longer, they'd likely have taken it.

A certain cohesion emerged within Stockdale's selected group. Taken as a whole, and due to the fact that there happened to be an unusually large number of officer school dropouts available, they were bright, resourceful men, with expectations of success. Many had an individualistic streak. Rusty Allen and Chris Mercer were among the anti-establishment types that emerged in the group--Rusty with a wink, Chris with impatience and cynicism.

More significant, though, than any common personality or background trait was the fact that this was one of the few scout-dog training units, and indeed the final one, from which the men came over together as an intact unit—not as individual replacements—and also one of the only units to bring to Vietnam the very dogs they had trained with at Fort Benning. They were all new together.

As they stepped out of the C-141 Starlifters and into the blinding, pungent atmosphere at Tan Son Nhut, the men couldn't have envisioned the changes they would undergo in Vietnam. Changes that might leave no visible mark would transform the men who handled the dogs. Combat would change them, of course. Their innocence would leave them forever. And having shared those defining moments of brutality and truth with their dog, the dog would also change them, and in an equally profound and fundamental way.

********

Months earlier, coincidental with the first days of the

47th's scout-dog training at Fort Benning, the North Vietnamese had launched the Tet offensive, a precision-planned, time-released series of uprisings across South Vietnam. Though it devastated NVA forces, it also succeeded in throwing U.S. strategy into disarray. This was the point at which the American public began to question our presence there in earnest, and to shift away from supporting the war.

Shortly after Tet, the men reported to their barracks for scout dog training, settling into the scrubby pines, soft sandy soil, and red clay of western Georgia, and into the woods, swamps, and sparse, brittle grass of their training area at the outer reaches of the vast Fort Benning complex. Here they got their first inklings of what scout dogs might be like in lectures and training films. They saw what the dogs could accomplish, and what part they themselves would be playing in those accomplishments.

By the third day, the call came to choose a dog, and suddenly it all came to life--their attention shifted to a living, breathing animal with needs, abilities, energy, and, possibly, a mind of its own. While they couldn't have had the full sense of the importance of the choice, they knew they were doing more than picking out a rifle or flack jacket.

The newly formed training class stood in tense formation in their clean, pressed fatigues, as a training sergeant looked them up and down, pacing deliberately, excruciatingly slowly in order to sharpen their anxiety, their eagerness. "When I give the word, all youse run down to the kennel area and stand outside the kennel door of the dog you want for your own." Moment of silence. The boot leather creaking, as press, press, press, he paced again. He stopped, back impossibly rigid.

"Okay, GO."

What would they look for in the animal? How could they tell which dog would be best at keeping its wits, staying the course, listening to them, keeping them alive? Should the dog be large and look ferocious? But the dog was not there to intimidate the enemy. The dog and the enemy shouldn't even witness one another by sight. The dog should find the man or men or bomb or toe popper or punji pit well before ever encountering the face of the enemy. That was the hope. So you needed to find a dog that had the best senses--the sharpest ears and nose, the quickest mind. How would you ever judge any of that in a mad dash down a line of chain-link kennels with forty or fifty other guys all hoping to find that perfect dog, and all the dogs barking, sharp and frantic, lunging at the gates of their kennels, somehow appearing to know just what was about to happen, and calling out, Choose me! Choose me! Even if you had all day and were by yourself, how would you know the right dog just by glancing at it? And everything you had, all your past and especially all your possibilities, could hinge on the choice of that animal.

They'd never been to Vietnam, and most hoped it would forever remain that way. But there it was, hanging out there, with all its terrible mystery. Facing the escalation of the war, at least one of the men, Rusty Allen, had doubted that they would even be allowed to remain in Georgia long enough to complete their training. At the same time, word of negotiations for possible peace talks would occasionally spike the air, giving the men hope that theirs would be a short stay in Southeast Asia. They would watch the news in the dayroom together, thinking, Will we be there?

21

Sometimes they would take a silent flight of hope when it looked like the politicians might get together and end the thing, but other times, standing around in small groups, they quietly discussed the possibility that they'd be sent over immediately. They would hear about bombing halts and Paris Peace Talks, then massive troop reinforcements. They would veer from hope to dread and back again weekly. The Army had made it clear that they could do anything with them that it pleased.

They had apprehensions enough to turn their selection of dogs into a frantic free-for-all sprint down to the kennels, each man planting himself in front of the kennel containing the dog he believed would see him home. In the midst of this chaos, they'd spot a possible match, then the dog would seem to slip away from their grasp. Somebody else got it, and each worried it might be better than the ones that were left. It was like choosing a bride from a book, or at a mad, mobbed college mixer, with only minutes, seconds to glance and envision a life together--the arguments and hilarity, the companionship and the irreconcilable differences. Till death or discharge, I thee wed.

Rusty Allen's youth in Texas had included dogs, and he felt he knew how to read them. He had a heavy thatch of strawberry-blond hair, snub nose, and wide-open eyes. Small, eager, quick, and cocky as a bantam rooster, he weighed only 115 pounds. After graduating from his Saratoga, Texas, high school in 1966, he worked first in a paper mill, then as a roughneck in the oil fields. In May of 1967 he was listed 1-A by the Texas draft board. Rusty's best friend, his fishing companion and co-conspirator in childhood adventures, his cousin Jimmy, was already in Vietnam.

He went through most of NCO school before being dropped, along with several others, for "lack of leadership" — or was it an unwillingness to conform? A percentage of each class had to fail anyway--to prove the program's rigor. Being picked up for scout dog school had seemed mildly intriguing; the days of orientation had pricked his curiosity further. Now he was as swept up in the excitement as the others, as they tore back and forth across the kennel aisles, trying to pinpoint the best dog for this new adventure. His choice was based on what he knew, dogs who had been pets or hunting companions.

He saw one that looked downcast but friendly, so he jumped into place by his gate. "Timber" was written on a small strip of tape on the run door. He was a medium-sized German shepherd with classic saddle markings. Rusty watched as an instructor moved down the line, easing each man inside his chosen dog's kennel. While some dogs defended their fenced territory with bared teeth, lunging at these intruders, defying them, Timber licked Rusty's hand through the fencing. *This is a baby,* thought Rusty, *the kind of dog you'd want at home lying curled up by the fireplace. If I have to go to Vietnam, this is the best way.*

Larry Proper had already been thinking that he wanted a dark-colored dog: he might be safer at night that way. Fellow had a brown spot over each eye, making him appear almost as if he had four eyes. *That's him. That's the one.* And then the sergeant was there, pointing, over the barking and the yelling, to the cage. Proper could barely hear him.

"Now go on in, Proper."

Larry glanced at the sergeant, then back at the dog.

He stood there. "He's going to bite me. Look at him." A few cages from where he stood, Proper had witnessed John Carter's dog sink his teeth into Carter's thigh.

"If he's going to, he'll do it right away."

Larry imagined for an instant that he stood a good chance of being devoured by the animal, but he crept into the cage. And as he did, the enormous black dog leapt onto him, and, shoving him up against the side of the cage, began wildly licking his face and neck.

Kennel by kennel, each man made contact with his new partner, both sides of the partnership filled with the flush of energy, optimism, and trepidation that comes with the first steps of a new relationship--business, friendship, or love, and this one would be all three. From this moment on, no one was alone.

A few of them would have their dogs for only a few weeks. As commander of the unit, Lt. Stockdale would not go out on missions in Vietnam, but would administer the use of the teams from the base camp. He would undergo the training program to get a feel for what the men were undertaking, before concentrating on his duties.

Jonathan Wahl had Willie for three weeks before being named platoon clerk. Wahl, a Long Island native, had graduated from Fairleigh-Dickinson College in Rutherford, New Jersey, with a degree in accounting. Knowing he was about to be drafted, he enlisted in Officer Candidate School, expecting to select a position working in finance. After ten weeks of officer training, however, he was told, "The needs of the Army have changed," and he would be heading straight for an infantry platoon in Vietnam as a Second Lieutenant, a job, as the trainees darkly joked among themselves, with an average life span of about thirty seconds. North Vietnamese and Viet Cong targeted officers, and men would be instructed never to salute them in the field. Wahl dropped out of the program, and as clerk, he had secured a position that suited his punctilious nature.

Since John Carter was tapped to become veterinary technician, a sort of medic for dogs, he would not keep his training dog long. Carter was another New Yorker. He grew up in Queens, with little exposure to animals. His father worked for a bank on Wall Street and his mother was an office manager. John had been pre-med in college for a few years, a serendipitous fact that qualified him for the vet tech job, and kept him out of the field.

Carter would tend to the dogs while they were at base camp, checking their health and preparedness for missions, treating them for parasites, illnesses, and heatstroke, administering routine shots, and patching up minor wounds. For serious injuries, dogs were evacuated by helicopter, exactly like wounded men, and rushed to veterinary centers with more sophisticated facilities and certified veterinarians. Carter worked with his dog for a few weeks to become familiar with handling the animals. From then on, he stayed at the kennels, working with the staff veterinarian. Though vet techs were normally sent to Walter Reed Medical Center in Washington for training, as were regular medics, Carter received only on-the-job training.

******

The first two weeks of training were given over to learning the basic commands of heel, sit, stay, down, and come. The men and their new partners worked in small squads, circling again and again in the red dirt and hot sun, the men giving orders to the dogs, the commands drilled into them for day-long sessions, four hours a day, six days a week. Some dogs had been through the system, but most were green, often snapping, snarling, recalcitrant pupils to their new handlers. For the many who had been rejected as pets, this may have been their first structured environment. Some were so aggressive and uncooperative that it took time for the handlers to learn to control them. Dogs were sometimes recycled through the system because they hadn't done well with an earlier class, or, as in Sig's case, because they performed so beautifully they became excellent training dogs. They could set the standard for a class.

Within those early weeks, important transformations were already underway. Awakening to the presence of their handlers, the dogs began responding to their commands. And the handlers were waking also, to a confidence in themselves--born of the knowledge that they were transforming the dogs--as well as in the dogs. Here was the beginning of mutual understanding, the first tender shoots of friendship between the dogs and their men, with the surprises, joys, and frustrations that define the early stages of companionship. Some of the teams, however, would not survive the process.

Early in training, two of the men found problems with their dogs. Jim Powrzanas's Sarge seemed off--he wanted to sleep continuously, and he was sluggish in class. "Why does he just sit there, looking dumb?" Jim asked a training sergeant. "He never gets excited about anything." Was Jim not up to the job, or was the dog inadequate? Powrzanas, at first embarrassed and frustrated, grew increasingly concerned about the well being of the dog.

Equally worrisome, Rusty found the endearing Timber skittish. While he'd mastered the basic skills adeptly, the dog was "soft," sensitive, in his overall personality. Rusty noticed that Timber would wince or cringe when the instructor shouted out commands. How would Timber hold up in a combat situation? Rusty was torn between his burgeoning attachment to the dog and the realities that faced him. Would further training strengthen the dog's confidence enough to enable him to endure the pressures of this work, or would Rusty be putting his own life, and the lives of a platoon of infantrymen, in jeopardy if he depended on the dog? Rusty was told to keep at it.

Sarge, on the other hand, tested positive for heartworms. He would not make it past the first training segment. A common problem in the south even today, and a major obstacle for the dogs working in Vietnam, heartworms enter the bloodstream as larvae by means of a mosquito bite. They settle in the heart, and can grow to nearly a foot in length. They obstruct blood flow and endanger the arteries as they join the heart. Symptoms include fatigue, a chronic cough, and weight loss. Sarge was pulled from duty, and Jimmy got a new dog, Pal.

Pal was a seventy-five-pound ball of energy. His coloring was somewhat unconventional--butterscotch mask, sweeping dark saddle, and caramel belly and legs; his longer legs and fine facial structure were also not within AKC standards. Coincidentally, though, many of these physical characteristics were reflected in Powrzanas himself, who was slender, fine-featured, and toffee-blond.

The two hit if off right away. Powrzanas admired his

dog's aggressiveness and smarts: "He's making me look like a pro," he joked with his friend Proper. Pal was happy and eager to work, but had an inexplicable attachment to his food bowl that never altered. Powrzanas had to use a rake to get it out of his kennel. Pal was high-strung in the best sense of the term. Quick, edgy, attentive, hardworking, and smart, he was ideally suited to the work of a scout dog. The pride Powrzanas took in the dog reflected a closeness, an identification, the men were beginning to feel with their dogs. If the dog performed well, the man performed well, because they were a unit now. The men were starting to embrace the dogs as part of themselves.

The dogs learned their basic commands through the classic choke-collar method--lavish praise for correct behavior, brisk jerk to the collar when they'd gotten it wrong. That was the jumping off point. The training would proceed from there, as the men themselves earlier had moved from basic to advanced and beyond. The dogs acquired a battery of skills, especially object and personnel detection, at increasingly difficult levels, and finally headed into field work, applying those skills to simulated war conditions. They would learn not only to find things--weapons, food, traps, people--but to distinguish between those things. And then the dog learned how to tell his handler just what it was he had found, so that it became a matter of mastering sometimes subtle and, the handler hoped, silent methods of communicating his knowledge.

For this phase of the training, the dog graduated from the choke collar to a leather harness. The neck was freed up, the harness running over the shoulders and under the chest. The dog would now learn that the minute the harness was attached to his body, work was at hand. This was the signal, the workday whistle. When work ended, the choke was slipped back on, and day was done. The dogs quickly learned to recognize their roles, their alternate personas.

Since the dog is only half of the team, the handler had to be trained as well as the dog, or better. The man was there to be the leader of the dog and the dog's interpreter. The instructors had to train the men to train the dogs.

"We've got an expression here," a trainer told them. "'It goes down the leash.' As training goes on, you'll see. It starts with the handler and moves down the leash to the dog. Eventually, you can almost know the man from watching the dog."

Sergeant Mendez had set the tone for the men from the beginning, "We train for go, not show," he told them. "If you want to be a dog handler, you'll probably make it. We'll work extra hours, weekends, do remedial work, or send you back through basic obedience again if you're having trouble getting it right. But for those who don't care, who are uninterested in working closely with a dog, those are the ones we reject. And there have been very few."

How many of these men would make it through? They'd latched onto their dogs in ways that had surprised even themselves.

As senseless as the war may have seemed to them, what they were doing now did have some sense to it. As dog handlers, they weren't going out to kill people. They were going out to guide and warn infantry, guys like themselves, about the ones who were out there to get *them*. They were out there to save the lives of our guys.

They were also going out to seek the enemy sometimes too, but at least any killing would be defensive. And they knew that when they were out there, they'd be walking in front of the infantrymen. "Here I get put into this dog training," Larry Proper reflected, "and suddenly I find I'm a professional point man." They would have to believe in their dog.

Even now, there was something inexplicably comforting in this animal. Already this was farther from home than they'd ever been, and so the dog was, for some, a little piece of familiarity, a souvenir of home life. As lousy as it felt to get up in the morning when you wanted to be asleep, the dogs were always thrilled to see you stepping out toward their kennel cage. They lived for you and you alone. How could you resist their enthusiasm? Work was joy, work was life, to the dogs. And as the men continued to see the dogs responding in training, they began to belong to the dogs too. There was, though, always that nagging near-certainty, *We two will be going to Vietnam soon unless something very, very lucky happens.*

Grating on the rest of them was lanky, swan-necked Marvin Pearce's gung-ho attitude. Of all the men, he was the only one who couldn't wait to get there. Pearce yearned to see action, experience combat. He had begged his parents in Capitola, California, a tiny resort town on Monterey Bay, to fill out the special-permission papers needed for him to enlist at age seventeen, when he was barely old enough to have a driver's license. He'd been rotating through a series of training programs in order to reach his eighteenth birthday, when he would be of age to be shipped overseas into the war zone. He passed that mark, but the Army still hadn't sent him. He would turn nineteen in March of 1968, midway through scout-dog training. He applied himself earnestly to every task, and he hoped.

******

Scouts are specialized scenters. While tracking dogs such as bloodhounds and retrievers pick up scent from ground or objects, scout dogs snatch the scent out of the air itself. The odor from an object dissipates into the air in a cone from the source, and is shaped by the existing air pattern. The scent is most intense at the source, the apex of the cone, then emanates outward, becoming increasingly diluted as the area of scent widens. The wind behind the source determines the direction and size of the cone, "like water breaking around a rock," explained Sergeant Mendez. In Europe during World War II the wide-open fields had provided too much area for the scent, allowing it to dissolve too quickly, so scout dogs hadn't been useful there. The terrain of Vietnam suited the talents of scout dogs somewhat better--low brushy areas, jungle trails, knobby fields, grassy dikes surrounding rice paddies, even river edges and villages. Conditions were tricky, though, and the weather conspired against them.

What made air-scent reading difficult: relentless floods of rain that lasted days or weeks and beat the scent down and out of the air (a light mist, though, held the scent), twisted trails in the jungles that interfered with scent traveling through air, and capricious wind currents swirling around mounds and valleys. Other general troublemakers that interfered with detection included heat, fatigue, snakes, parasites, and NVA and

Viet Cong expertise at diffusing or disguising scents.

The average distance that dogs detected personnel in Vietnam was about 200 meters, though in ideal conditions an alert could occur at twice that, and alerts could range to 1,000 meters. Even twenty to thirty meters, though, typical under jungle conditions, would allow the men adequate time to prepare themselves, so conditions did not need to be ideal. The dogs were able to find boobytraps buried underground, hidden in water, or concealed in trees--that had lain there for hours, days, or even months. Because they detect the chemical emitted by the explosive, not the device itself, they made the use of electronic mine detectors, dependent on metal for any effectiveness, seem primitive. In practice, dogs were faster at detection, and the electronic detectors gave more false alarms.

All of the dogs' senses contributed to their abilities as scouts. Dogs can hear at four times the distance that man is able to; and those dogs who, like German shepherds, also have broad, mobile ears are better equipped to find and collect those sounds. Scout dogs were also employed for their ability to navigate in the darkness, which is not only what occasionally happened at night, but what the day could look like in the jungle. Dogs can see objects at greater distances than man--up to a mile--if the object is moving, hence the freeze instinct of prey animals such as rabbits and deer. Additionally, dogs have a field of vision that extends about 250 degrees, as opposed to ours at 180 degrees. Their depth of field isn't as accurate as ours, so they sometimes have trouble judging distances or finding something seemingly right under their noses. And though the old belief that dogs see only in black and white has been disproved, the fact remains that sight is less important to a dog than some of his other senses.

But it is the dog's sense of smell that outperforms all the others. Dogs' scenting ability, that amazing nose, is something that even today we don't fully understand.

The debate about how much "better" the dog's scenting ability is than our own is superfluous. The average dog has 220 million olfactory receptor cells in his nose whizzing messages to the olfactory bulb in the canine brain, while we have five million; he has seven square meters of nasal membrane tightly folded into that long nasal cavity, to imbibe, decode, and relay smells, compared to our one-half meter. A dog retains his scent memories for his entire life. A scenting sample: the pebble test. Six subjects are given a pebble each. They hold the pebble briefly, then throw it as far as they're able. A dog smells one of the subjects' hands and is sent in the direction of the pebbles. He is able to find the pebble that was handled by the subject whose hand he smelled. The chemical given off by human sweat, butyric acid, is the identifying factor. The only way to confuse a dog about an individual human's scent is to present him with identical twins: fraternal twins will provide as two scents; identical twins, one.

In tests such as these, dogs were found to have about the same scenting ability on flowers as humans, but in detecting butyric acid, it was conclusively proven that they did indeed have an ability exceeding our own by one million times. Enemy hiding in the sweltering jungles of Vietnam would involuntarily call out to the dogs with their body scent, each an individual odor to the dog.

Officer Carl A. Newcombe, director of the detector

dog program of the U.S. Customs Service, has also found that puppies raised in foster homes before entering the program make far better detectors than those raised in kennels. Human companionship, especially in a sense- and skill-enriching environment such as the scout dogs enjoyed, increases the level of the dog's abilities. Dogs' senses are heightened, and their overall quality of being elevated, by their association with humans in such a stimulating environment. This is expressed by dog behaviorist Dr. Bruce Fogle: "His mind functions according to the information it receives from his senses....The more sensory information that the dog's brain receives, the more developed his mind will become. Anatomically speaking, sensory stimulation causes nerve cells in the brain to actually grow and make new synaptic connections with other nerve cells. The network expands to accommodate and assimilate new information." Training would be the beginning.

The nose is connected to the brain, not a battery or an engine. The dog had to process the information that the nose, ears, and eyes brought into the brain. And then the dog had to react to the information. During that connection, judgment occurs, a decision results. But how much is up to the individual's intelligence and how much is just instinctive or reflexive reaction? During obstacle courses in training, for example, some dogs made the decision to remain inside the cool tunnel, defying orders and wisely lowering their body temperature. Was this sense or instinct? Regardless, the ploy was trained out of those who tried it.

The men were fast realizing that it was a thinking brain, and that they would be depending on the signal they got from the dog to tell a platoon of men just what they should be doing to keep everybody alive. The handlers were discovering a new kind of empathy. They were learning to put themselves inside their dog's mind in order to see what the dog had heard, to hear what the dog had smelled. They would have to know their dog perfectly, to know when to accept their dog's opinion and interpretation of things; that is, they were learning how to trust an animal.

*****

Pearce reveled in the training, strutting in his fresh fatigues with head cocked, cleaning his weapon perhaps too often and just a little too carefully. Secretly, he kept with him a .38-caliber revolver and a large hunting knife, his personal weapons. His mother, barely literate yet confident in carriage, had smuggled them into the barracks on a visit. She had wanted to be sure her "boy" was safe. Our own little John Wayne, the others grumbled. Marvin's middle name was Robert. He wanted to drop the "Marvin," and recast himself as "Bob." Bob Pearce, he would whisper to himself, sounds like Army. The men ignored it, and only called him "Pearce." But silently, and surprised, they were coming to recognize that the connection between Pearce and his dog was growing just as true as anyone's.

Pearce provided the conditions needed for the bond to develop with Prince, his large, blond dog, even if he hadn't succeeded as well with the men. On that frantic day of choosing a partner, Pearce had sought a bold, macho dog. He'd wanted a dog that, like his military equipment, would cloak him in the images of masculinity that were his fantasy. Though Prince had been a handful at first, Marvin had steadily risen to the challenge. He put in extra training hours, sometimes asking Rusty for help. He wanted to get it right. And this time with the dog began effecting some small changes inside him as well. He could feel something when he saw the changes in the dog. And the dog looked to him for leadership. No one had done that before.

Rusty was finding something else altogether in his dog. He was now certain that he would not be able to trust Timber. The dog was gun shy, as continued exposure to battle sounds made increasingly clear. Bolting at each pop of training explosive, Rusty could barely hang onto him in the field. Timber was not going to become a scout dog. With fortuitous timing, Sig became available when the lieutenant who would head the 47th's sister platoon, the 59th, gave up the dog to assume fulltime administrative duties.

One of the largest of the dogs, "the giant," Otis Johnson called him, Sig was well suited to become Rusty's partner. Both man and dog were vivacious, sandy-haired, and about the same weight: At 105 pounds, Sig nearly matched Rusty. In the relationship there was a synchronistic spark, and Rusty was at home with the dog at once. He immediately recognized the difference between his affection for Timber and this meeting of minds. A pet was an animal you'd love and coddle, and who would comfort you. That was one thing, and it was wonderful, too, life-enriching. But he could see in Sig suddenly the possibility of something else--a force to be reckoned with, a smart, independent spirit. A working, mutual respect had begun.

And what of the dogs? Did they also recognize qualities in the men? Do dogs understand when their handler is trying to tap into their mind? The instructors continually told them, "The closer you get to your dog, the better the dog will work, and the greater your chances of survival." There were the basics: each man fed and groomed his own dog each day, and cleaned his dog's kennel run, duties they would continue throughout the partnership. It was part of the foundation for the bond. And the men also began to spend as much extra time with their dogs as their instructors would allow. There they would find themselves developing that other, less defined sort of connection.

As training advanced, they moved over trails that simulated the Vietnamese environment, except they were in sandy-floored, pine forests. The trails included hidden pits, except without the sharpened sticks of a true punji pit. If a dog fell into one of these practice pits, it happened only once. Having learned that the pits existed, they avoided them, walking deliberately off the trail around them. They were expert at detecting them in Vietnam, nearly always confounding the handler at the far end of the leash. The handler thought the trail was just as it looked; the pits were flawlessly concealed, with "not a teaspoon of dirt out of place," as Nathaniel Tripp put it in his Vietnam memoir.

Because of the pits, and the other dangers they were learning to detect and avoid, this was the time when they began hearing the instructors' mantra: Walk where the dog walks, always walk where the dog is walking, follow his steps one by one. Let go of yourself, your thinking self, open your senses, and place your trust in the dog. The dog was supposed to stop in front of the pit to let you know it was there; but often they were too far into their job to interrupt themselves, and simply led their handler where he should go, believing he would follow.

The dogs were exposed to more battle noises of automatic fire and explosives. They went up for helicopter rides. They searched mock villages--a job that would prove difficult for them in Vietnam because of the temptation to rout chickens  or pigs or buffaloes or fellow dogs or cats, and because of the tendency to alert on village families as well as Viet Cong. Obstacle courses heightened the dogs' agility and endurance. They learned to crawl low to the ground alongside their handlers, a tactic that, if they remembered it, would save their lives when they were caught in ambushes.

At each level of training, instructors made sure to engage the interest of the dog, adding human decoys, dummy explosions, mixing up the routine, whatever it took to keep it exciting. When a dog knows too well what's coming, he gets bored and loses his effectiveness as a worker. Imagination was required in training the dogs. If they were overly tired, as sometimes happened in Vietnam when missions went on longer than planned, the dogs' senses would shut down, jeopardizing the men. So on longer missions, units were allowed to take two scout dog teams, which they could alternate. Fatigue made them vulnerable, though often the dogs, after a full day of patrolling, would either be put or put themselves on guard duty through the night.

They were not trained to attack people, but these weren't dogs you could cuddle up to unless, of course, you were the beloved handler. Nor were the dogs friendly to the other dogs. A pack identity did not form among them. Wouldn't the fact that they were lined up side by side, day after day, in the kennel runs, and trained together every day have created a unified corps? It didn't--dogs got injured in fights all the time, in training and in Vietnam. The pack that did exist consisted of one man and one dog.

As tight as these individual man-dog units became, there was an adaptive, though variable, flexibility as well. Chris Mercer's first dog hadn't worked out, so he was assigned a new one, Dusty, a strong, sharp-faced dog.

Like Pearce, Mercer came from Northern California, but that was their only common ground. Mercer had enjoyed a privileged upbringing, even if had not been able to elude the draft as so many others from his background had done. Chris landed in NCO school, and every day he woke up astonished to find himself still there. He resented everything about the military, and had been bounced, along with Rusty, out of even the indignity of NCO school, where he'd built a reputation as a troublemaker. He did have friends within the group, those whose previous lives most resembled his own, the "college boys." But despite his antipathy, he found he liked working with the dogs.

Chris was ready for Dusty, but Dusty, who had been Lt. Stockdale's dog for several months, became confused. In Vietnam, dogs would routinely receive new handlers as their earlier ones rotated out or were injured. The transition normally took a few days to a few weeks, and if the former handler was still in the camp, he would be told to stay well clear of the dog. The former handler was physically gone, and having no leader, most of the dogs would quickly look to and accept the new handler.

But Dusty had bonded stubbornly to Stockdale. Now he was expected to respond to Mercer, with Stockdale still present, and Dusty was having none of it. Sig hadn't had a problem attaching himself to Rusty. Maybe Sig was a quicker learner, or just more flexible mentally. But Dusty resisted, and the transition was tough for all involved. Mercer would have to draw deeply into his sense of leadership and confidence, and work consistently, attentively until the dog understood. And he did, and the dog eventually responded. He came to recognize Mercer as his other, himself, and the bond ultimately became seamless. Dusty was a strong attacher, and the two developed the ability to get inside one another.

******

For the final segment of training, the men lived in tents in the woods, as close as they could get to actual conditions of a long-range patrol. They were sent out on simulated missions, where they would integrate all phases of their training, and encounter the stiffest challenges yet, individually and as teams.

They lived in the field and worked their mock missions in the heat to what they then believed was the point of exhaustion. One dog-man team would take the point position, while the others followed, acting as the infantry platoon. Those who followed the point team would also build endurance, gain exposure to potential situations, and witness explosions and gunfire.

Among those who had fallen into a close working relationship with his dog was Jonathan Harraden. Despite his black dog's early menacing demeanor, and the fact that he was a large, bulky dog while Harraden was a small, wiry man, Jonathan liked Dawg. He enjoyed the streak of outlaw in his dog. Training had gone well and the two had melded into a solid unit. Only toward the end of this period did the knot nearly unravel.

This was a night mission. Someone else had the point and they'd been walking a couple of hours. The dog at point alerted, ears and tail up, hackles raised. The handler lifted his arm in silent warning. The men and dogs froze. Then the "get down" signal from the handler. Harraden lowered himself, pulling as he did on Dawg's choke collar. But instead of joining Harraden, moving as one with him as he normally did, Dawg, with teeth clenched, let a quiet growl roll out of one side of his mouth: he was tired, and he didn't want to lie down in the mud and sticks. It was the first time he'd tested his handler. Surprised, Harraden shoved the dog into a prone position next to him.

They continued on. But then, the next time an alert was given, the dog resisted again. This time the growl was harsher, the snarl hoisted high, the teeth flashing white against the night and the dark coat of the dog. Harraden knew he was being challenged now, and for real. This was where the smarts of the man, tired or not, would have to prove unequivocally to the dog that the dog must obey.

In one smooth movement, Harraden stood, shook the leash loop from his hand, and tossed it over a thick pine branch above his head. Then, sharply, he grabbed the end of the leash with both hands and pulled--as if sounding a hundred-pound church bell--lifting the startled and now barking and flailing dog off of the ground, effectively hanging him in the air by his choke collar.

He hung the dog for about three seconds. Then he lowered him to the ground and walked away.

This technique of hanging a dog for several seconds to assert dominance is a bonafide component of the methods of William R. Koehler, whose training manual first came out in 1962, and remains in print today. While the idea seems unnecessarily harsh in light of current training methods, Harraden knew that he was heading for a place where there could be no doubt of who called the moves. The dog would not challenge Harraden again.

As far as he and the others in the unit were concerned, abuse was out of the question. By this time, late in the training, they'd developed an intimate bond that precluded the possibility. Hanging was not done out of anger; it was a training technique, a way of subduing dogs that could be dangerously aggressive. They knew that their own authority must be indelibly etched onto the dogs' minds. Their lives, and the lives of the men they would lead on missions, depended on it.

The handlers, who'd all been trained to use the technique, were taught that it didn't really hurt the dog, that dogs had sturdy, muscular necks unlike our own, and they'd never seen a dog injured by it. It was sometimes used during the early phases of training, when the men had needed to establish the leadership role in their dogs' eyes. John Carter had been ordered to a similar action, known as helicoptering, in his first days of training. When his dog tried to get the better of him, the training officer commanded, "Carter, hand up that dog and give him a ride." So the soft-spoken, gentle-handed Carter lifted the eighty-five-pound animal and swung him from the end of the leash until there was no fight remaining in him, and both dog and handler were exhausted.

The dogs were never to be struck by a handler. War-dog historian Michael Lemish concurs that dogs in the military were well treated; no one would be allowed to abuse them. The military was investing time and money in the acquisition, processing, feeding, housing, and training of the animal. It served their interest to keep the dog healthy and well adjusted. Most important, abusive treatment would set up a fear-based form of obedience, and the dog could one day turn around on the handler. Beating might subdue a dog, but would not guarantee his loyalty. And he wouldn't know if your raised hand was about to punish or praise him. The hand should only be used in praise. The dog would work for you because he understood and trusted completely in the bond, and because he wanted to please you. They had to think as one, never as adversaries.

Hanging the dog for a few seconds shocked and frightened the dog, and rendered him helpless. The usual way to do it was to hold their arms out and briefly lift the dog up until he quieted his aggression.

43

This, to most people, cruel act, and the detached way in which the men executed it, speaks to the experience of war: Young men barely out of their teens, if that, who are training to find people who are waiting to kill them, find the act of briefly hanging a dog by his neck acceptable. It represented a choice of life over death. Though they may not have intended to be soldiers, they were now, and they were assimilating a culture of violence, preparing for an environment of brutality. They would enter this existence together, and it would bind them together forever.

******

Graduation day grew near, and the men continued their march toward Vietnam. They had one final hurdle, the Operational Readiness Test. And they did want to be ready. The anticipation of going to Vietnam ate away at them, for now there weren't going to be any impediments to their going over, and they knew it.

To be completed within forty-eight hours, the test would place them in the simulated conditions that they'd been rehearsing. The object: to test their "combat readiness."

They would first demonstrate "establishing a tactical assembly area," choosing an area suitable for staking out the dogs for several days, providing appropriate camouflage and security, feeding and care of the dogs, maintaining equipment, and "rending reports," writing it all up, Army style. Four hours were then allotted to set up and show their skills on training lanes, with booby traps and three human decoys each.

In part two, which was to last five hours, each scout

dog team would lead a platoon on a daytime patrol. Umpires would check their preparation--if, for example, all metal parts on the dogs' equipment were taped to prevent noise as they walked--their ability to detect snipers and hidden personnel, as well as mantraps, boobytraps, and equipment.

Part three recreated nighttime operations and lasted about ten hours. Teams were placed on outpost positions as well as patrols and would need to exhibit early detection of enemy, boobytraps, and arms. In the final ten-hour segment, each team would support a road- or trail-clearing operation. The dogs would be fed and rested; the men checked for accomplishing that, plus the sanitation and security of the assembly area. At the end of the test, equipment, weapons, and vehicles were also inspected. Those who failed the test would likely be sent to Vietnam anyway, but as regular infantrymen.

At the May 3, 1968, graduation Captain John McCune, who presided over the event, announced that the class had scored uniformly above average on the test. Several of the dog-man teams had been ranked Outstanding. And Rusty, with his smart-mouthed swagger, had earned the title of Honor Graduate: He and Sig had achieved the near impossible, a perfect score.

The frustrations with the Army--the draft, the age limit, the endless details and senseless procedures, the whimsies of authority--that had led them into scout dog training were behind them, and the day nearly all of them had dreaded was at hand.

The official, typed list with the names of those going overseas, in alphabetical order and according to rank, was distributed to the men. Some names were missing: a precious few had had the luck or the connections to be pulled out and placed in other, stateside programs. Jonathan Wahl's best friend throughout training became a clerk at the training school. Mercer checked the list with a flicker of hope. But there he was, on the line just above Jim Powrzanas.

Scanning eagerly, Marvin Pearce searched out his own name, which should have been between Mercer and Powrzanas. It was not there. He fled to Otis, who did find it--out of order and at the bottom of the page. Confused and crushed, Pearce saw he was listed conditionally, as a "standby" member of the 47th. The one among them who wanted to go to war would only travel to Vietnam if someone else, for some unknown reason, became unable to make the flight.

Otis waved his broad hand, ever-present cigarette between index and third fingers, over the list. "No way are you not coming, Pearce." He wanted Pearce to be there. He knew Pearce was a willing worker. A natural and unhesitating leader, Otis offered to speak to someone; this must be a clerical error. But Pearce was worried. He'd been passed over before.

Their stateside training now complete, the men were given two weeks to set their affairs in order before their flight to the Republic of Vietnam.

---

Notes

30,000 draft/month of Aug. 67: Dougan, p. 197.

Number of troops: *Encyclopedia of American History*, p. 497.

The 47th IPSD had existed in World War II and was reactivated on January 2, 1968. *47Th IPSD Commander's Briefing.*

From an email from Michael G. Lemish, "In 1968, there were 650 Army scout dogs and 59 Marine scout dogs. Toss in the Army sentry and trackers, along with the Air Force, and you probably had about 1300 total." 9/30/99.

Some men were totally unsuited to dog handling, but were sent to that position anyway. John Delware, who was with the training unit at Ft. Benning, the 26th IPSD, in 1969, told me this: "I worked very hard at getting three people reassigned while I was there. I had a professional sous-chef from a famous restaurant in New Orleans who was deathly afraid of dogs. I suggested that the Army could use his talents in the mess hall. They disagreed and he dropped out of the dog program to become an infantry grunt. I had a Ph.D. research chemist who was trying to get to Walter Reed Army Hospital. Again the Army knew better and left him to the dogs. The third was a man who was so terrified of dogs he went AWOL, and when he returned, he suffered a mental breakdown. When I was told to empty his locker and ship his stuff out, I found a large black snake, his pet and according to him the only who he was ever able to talk his problems over with." email of 11/8/99.

The method of selection varied from class to class, depending on who was doing the training, since they'd begun sending scout dogs over for American use in 1966. In some places I've read that the dogs were assigned to handlers (not selected in this helter-skelter method), to ensure the optimum personality match, but in this instance, the dogs were chosen by the handlers.

The 47th and 59th were supposed to be the last units sent over intact, but the 60th IPSD was sent to Vietnam from April to October 1969.

Though policies at different times and among individual commanders varied, it was standard practice to evacuate injured dogs as needed during the time covered in this book.

Skills v. conditions in Vietnam, including blindfolded hearing: Densford, p. 29 ff.

Staying in tunnel: Martin, p. 41.

Tripp, p. 105.

*Operations Readiness Test*, Dept. Of the Army Publications, June 1968, courtesy of Jesse Mendez.

*Infantry Scout Dog Graduation of Class #3*, 3 May 1968, brochure, courtesy of Bert Hubble.

---

Captions

p. 36: Rusty Allen and Sig.

p. 38: Otis Johnson and Rolf.

pp. 45-47: Infantry Scout Dog Graduation, May, 1968.

# Omen

Flying west from Georgia, a few grabbed the webbed seats strung inside the shell of the plane, while the others draped themselves where there was space--across the vehicles, beside dog crates, along the floor. Lieutenant

Stockdale opened his orders, and learned their destination. It was real now, and he quietly announced it to the others. Most were silent.

"Right on, man. A righteous outfit. Hundred and *First.*" Pearce had made the flight after all. An incident in the town of Columbus had opened the way for him: a rowdy night of bar hopping had led to the arrest of one of the men scheduled for the flight. That soldier would await his trial there, and find his way to Vietnam later. But suddenly a slot was open, and Pearce finally got the nod. He was elated. The 101st was an elite division, whose reputation fueled his daydreams of war. Now he would be one of them.

The others were thinking, These guys are already known to be aggressive and tough, and they will call up a dog team in situations that they find difficult.

Jim and Larry met eyes. In the way he had of steadying the sensitive Proper, Jim leaned into Larry's

shoulder, glancing toward Pearce,

"Go git'em, cowboy."

These two had become friends during training. Powrzanas's quickness and low-key geniality complemented Proper's quiet, gentle earnestness, and they shared a maturity that set them apart. When they had received their draft notices, Jim was working at the Birmingham, Alabama, airport servicing small planes, and Larry was in tiny Meadville, Pennsylvania, at the Erie-Lakawanna Railroad, apprenticed to a carman, and holding every expectation of eventually becoming a foreman. Each had thought that he would remain with his employer for life, but the draft would cut short both careers. Both had been married shortly before leaving for training, and both, in a matter of months, would become long-distance fathers.

Stockdale studied the name of their location and checked his map. LZ Sally was in the northern part of South Vietnam. As he traced the tinted calligraphic map lines with a dry pink fingertip, straining through the odd names--names that would  soon trip off his tongue: Phu Bai, Thua Thien, Quang Tri, Song Bo, Dong Ha--to determine what lay around this destination, he found other names he recognized a little too easily—the Demilitarized Zone, the A Shau Valley, Khe Sanh, and the Ho Chi Minh Trail.

Missions for the 47th would take them west onto that trail, north across the DMZ, and east and southeast toward and through Hue and to the edges of the China

Sea. Because of their northern location, the 47th would be dealing with NVA troops more than VC. NVA were tougher, more skilled, and tenacious than the VC recruits. The area essentially belonged to the North Vietnamese. This was I Corps, with its heavy-breathing jungles, iron-leached, red-rocky mountain trails, brushy lowlands, soggy rice fields, and blistering sandy dunes, and it was to be their home, among the most dangerous areas of the country, at the height of our engagement there.

When they landed at Elmsdorf Air Force Base, Alaska, to refuel, it was night and cold. They walked the dogs and then ate a dinner of spaghetti in the mess hall. Afterward they reboarded and tried again to sleep. Repeat at Yokata Air Force Base, an even shorter stop. Closer came their final stop.

At last descending to Tan Son Nhut, their jumpy stomachs were assuaged by the sheer beauty of the place. Lush blue-green-purple foliage like an iridescent, undulating curtain of velvet, sparkling with rice-paddy jewels, rosette treetops bursting above the forests, straining in the fecundity to reach the sunlight. Invisible was the undergrowth that festered and grew from the dampness within those jungled mountains. Best just to absorb this sight, not think what it was, what was in it, who was in there waiting for them. No one noticed that silence had enveloped them, as each drew into himself, alone with the shock of this unexpected beauty.

John Carter, pushing away images of his distracted goodbye kiss to Sue, a see-ya-later buss in the surreal moment of separation, eyed the random ponds sprinkled among the green, the paddies, the open areas, and he tried to feel as calm as their liquid surfaces appeared.

They were bomb craters, he would later learn, filled by rains to become ponds.

Rusty's mood quieted his jitters. When he'd arrived home on leave, those final two weeks before this flight, he'd gotten the worst news of his young life. His cousin Jimmy, gone to Vietnam a few months ahead of him, was killed in a firefight. He didn't like to look at it as a sign or as bad luck. It was horrific, a loss he couldn't yet calculate, but he would endure it, and it wouldn't happen to him. He trusted in his own lucky streak.

Despite the long journey, he'd kept himself looking relatively crisp and feeling his natural energy. He  fortified himself with the knowledge that he was walking in with some status: Like a door gunner or even a special forces man, a dog handler had prestige. He was more than a new grunt. He allowed himself even to beam a little, thinking how he would impress the infantry guys with his magnificent Sig. Dog handlers were indeed part of a specialized elite--in 1968 there were more than half a million American troops in Vietnam, but only about seven hundred scout dogs with handlers.

The others shared this sense of trepidation that mingled with confidence in their recently acquired expertise. As Stockdale had predicted, the men had come in with high standards. They had trained hard and well, mastering the new skills, demanding and receiving the best from their dogs, accepting them as their teammates. If they had to be there, they were ready to prove themselves. They were not cocky or eager, only ready.

But in a few hours they would have to discover how green they were after all. They would witness the weariness, sometimes the contempt, in the eyes of the used-up troops as they returned back from the countryside. The handlers may have been special troops, but they were brand spanking new special troops. The faces of the returning troops had been as fresh as the new handlers' were now, and those soldiers could just barely remember that innocent time. How would these handlers ever be like that?

The dogs were not quiet. As the men withdrew, each into his private search for fortitude, the dogs knew the game was finally at hand. Their barking and pacing escalated. Nails tapping, they skidded across the floors of their crates. And the crates smelled of two days of dog waste. Cleaning crates wasn't something the men normally looked forward to, but at this moment they did, wanting to expunge the smell.

That smell was faint perfume, though, compared with the stench of burning human excrement that greeted them as the belly of their plane opened. The smell and the heat sucked the breath out of them. Their eyes stung from the smell, the heat, the light, the dust. With lowered glances, they could see the spiny remains of the air traffic tower, and lower, the bullet-pocked buildings. The air was so laden with humidity that their clothes immediately drank in the dampness, and that wetness commingled with a sudden burst of nervous sweat. They tried to assume the faces of men under control.

As part of standard procedure, while Stockdale accompanied the men to Bien Hoa for in-country training, the dogs would remain at the veterinary center in Tan Son Nhut for a ten-day quarantine period. Stockdale put together some volunteers—incuding Rusty, Pearce, Jim Powrzanas, and John Carter-- to stay behind with the dogs.

The others, up in Bien Hoa, would begin to discover the realities of the Vietnam war environment, as opposed to stateside training--how they were hunted, what was out there, what worked in this terrain, what to forget from earlier training, what the weather did to their weapons and their own ability to function. And Jonathan Wahl, as platoon clerk, would add to the inventory another dog, a frisky, black-and-white female mongrel puppy. Now he would have a dog, too, a platoon mascot.

It was not unusual for men in any unit to pick up mascot pets, in this war and in all the others before it, who served quite apart from any military use. With mascots, social significance, not utility, matters. A dog can absorb those insecurities that cannot be mentioned. They can distract, amuse, and ultimately elevate the spirit, or at least the general tone surrounding the men. By their interest and subordination, mascots empower as well as comfort their keepers. A pet was something they could manage when everything else seemed overwhelmingly beyond their control. When you feel the ocean of fear and alienation surrounding you, there is one who looks up to you, needs you, and soothes you deep down. There is a human urge to pull an animal near in times of need. And even discounting the emotional ties, it's simply a fact that petting a dog lowers a person's blood pressure.

While dogs have always worked in wars, in a variety

of capacities, they've also always held that other role as mascot. As a symbol of the comforts of home, family, and familiarity, mascot dogs are well documented, for example, in Civil War sources. They are described in letters and journals, and included in photographs and etchings. As a first lieutenant in the Union Army, George Armstrong Custer posed for a photographer with a group camped at Cumberland Landing. Hatless, he lies across a blanket by a tent, propped on an elbow, jacket half-unbuttoned, gently stroking a mixed-breed dog that curls against his thick trousers. Serene, the lounging dog represents the antithesis of the horrors that surrounded him.

On the Gettysburg battlefield, there is a small statue commemorating the dog Sally, mascot for the 11th Pennsylvania Infantry. Sally was with the 11th Pennsylvania from puppyhood and served as unit mascot for several years. When she became separated from her unit during a retreat, she returned to the battlesite and remained with the dead until she was picked up by another unit, the 12th Massachusetts, which was able to reunite them.

Various Civil War mascot dogs were taught to perform military salutes, bob to camp songs, even hold a pipe in their teeth. They were also stolen from one another, a symbolic gesture that delighted the thieving side, as if a boyish prank. One dog, Jack, of the Volunteer Firemen of Niagara, Pennsylvania, was captured twice by the Confederates. He escaped his first incarceration. After the second capture, he was exchanged for a human Confederate prisoner. An odd act of whimsy, or human value placed on a mascot?

Confederate and Union troops alike kept dogs,

eagles, sheep, and other animals as pets. Mascots during the Vietnam war weren't limited to dogs either. The men adopted full grown eagles, roe deer, monkeys, bears, even tigers and pythons, and the American veterinarians and vet techs attended to them.

Mascots were not partners in the sense that the handlers' dogs were. They hadn't the same load to carry, though some did anyway.

A famous mascot of World War I, the mixed terrier Stubby, cheered men at the front lines in France, but like other mascots through the ages, also warned of incoming artillery and helped locate the wounded, though he had never been trained to do so.

In Vietnam, Paul Morgan's dog Suzi was not a military dog, but a forty-five-pound German shepherd-type who was living in the village of Cau Xang with a Vietnamese Catholic priest. The priest was an anti-Communist activist, and he kept Suzi as his gentle and beloved pet, and also quite effective bodyguard. Father Nguyen Cong Tu gave Suzi over to Morgan, who was a military advisor at the time, in a special ceremony, as thanks for his protection (Morgan also gave the priest some guns and a silver rosary). Though not a dog handler, Morgan kept the animal with him constantly, even tethered to his leg at night, during his 1965 advisory tour. In return she not only transferred her loyalty to him, but alerted him and his fellow soldiers to numerous hazards both in battle and at camp. At the end of his assignment, Morgan gratefully gave Suzi back to Father Tu.

Other mascots rose to these levels as well, but the role of mascot in and of itself was an important one, and now the 47th had theirs. She would belong to all of them (though maybe just a little more to Jonathan Wahl). She would not engender any rivalry. She had nothing to do with going out in to the field. She was benign. When they got her, the black and white puppy was about the size of an army field boot.

"What is this pitiful dog?" Otis rubbed the puppy's head. Otis had seen Wahl walking with the puppy and had come over to investigate. Something new was happening and Otis had a need to know--he was one of those whose interior radar system was always in action. He was also the sort who, even when reading a book, would constantly stop to comment out loud or share what he'd learned with those around him. "Listen to this, Rusty,..." He was ever outward-seeking. Appointed as a squad leader, this natural inclination grew protective. His senses reached around his men like a mantle. He showed, he talked, he kept things moving.

Wahl cocked a smile, "This is Flexible. In honor of Sprowl."

Otis liked that. Making a little fun of Sergeant Sprowl, who regularly admonished them to "remain flexible"--Sprowl's understanding of Army procedure, which meant to them, as to combat soldiers everywhere, random changes in orders, inexplicable duties and delays, endless boredom, and brief, terrifying flashes of frenzied action. And it leavened as well any sense of sentimentality that might have been surging at the sight of this tumble of puppy love.

******

At Tan Son Nhut, the men who had volunteered to stay with the dogs while they were quarantined reported to the 936th Veterinary Detachment, the main vet center in Vietnam. While platoons like the 47th had a vet tech, the full-fledged veterinarians were stationed at veterinary hospitals and food distribution centers throughout the countryside. (Most U.S. vets in Vietnam inspected food, for human as well as canine consumption.) The 936th at Tan Son Nhut, though, was the mother vet hospital, and it was through here that all military dogs entered the country.

U.S. dogs had been traveling to Vietnam since the early sixties, when Jesse Mendez came over to train the South Vietnamese to use scouts and sentries. The South Vietnamese never did get it right. It wasn't their custom to care for dogs as pets, much less train them as working animals, as they did with buffalo. Vietnamese veterinarians were virtually nonexistent. And since these feisty, unfamiliar dogs could easily outweigh the men, the South Vietnamese soldiers were afraid of them. When Mendez tried to train the South Vietnamese Army, known as the Army of the Republic of Vietnam, or ARVN, troops to use the dogs, they couldn't latch onto the concept of praising the effusive, burly animals. The entire undertaking seemed absurd and useless to them. And the food they were expected to feed these animals represented far richer rations than the troops themselves were allotted. Ninety percent of the dogs who died in the hands of the South Vietnamese died of malnutrition. In their culture, dogs might make an occasional meal, but not a friend to fight by their side.

The first dogs to support U.S. troops in Vietnam were sentry dogs assigned to airbases. They began arriving in 1965, shortly after the first U.S. troops themselves. After the attack at Danang, the military made sure of it. They also went to Bien Hoa and Tan Son Nhut to watch over those bases. By 1967, the Army was using a total of nearly 400 dogs, though by 1968 that number would nearly triple, including the 700 scout dogs. Tracking, mine-, and tunnel-detecting dogs, as well as off-leash scout dogs, would be phased in as the war progressed.

The biggest threats to these dogs were not the enemy, but other, non-human forces. Poor food, its storage and dispersal, which improved as the war continued, and accidents jumping into or out of helicopters or trucks were among the problems. But the harsh physical environment proved most dangerous, and those ten days of quarantine at Tan Son Nhut were invaluable in permitting the dogs to adapt to the climate.

The first U.S. military dog to die in Vietnam succumbed to heatstroke on an airbase tarmac, and that affliction would plague the dogs throughout the war, their main killer or crippler. Snakes were everywhere, as were parasites, internal and external, and these also threatened the dogs continually.

In 1967 a mysterious disease appeared and decimated the ranks of the dogs over the subsequent years. Dogs would develop a fever that lasted days or even weeks, then seem to recover completely. Several months later, they would begin bleeding from the nose, weaken rapidly, and die within days. A parasite was suspected, though not yet identified by the time the 47th arrived in the Republic of Vietnam. The disease was therefore called simply idiopathic hemorrhagic syndrome (IHS), and dipping and fumigating took place regularly.

The 936th vet detachment at Tan Son Nhut would

play the central role in attempting to cope with all of these threats. Still, it was not an elaborate setup: a couple of trailers for the staff's housing, and an evolving treatment and dispensary center, with dog runs at the side of the structure.

Rusty, Pearce, Jimmy, and John Carter sat around on flimsy chairs, kicking out their feet, waiting for the paperwork, waiting to hose down crates, to pour food into tins, to look after those dogs. Tonight they would sleep on the cool, hard concrete around the dog runs. There were no other accommodations available to them. They would be introduced to their off-base barracks—a filthy, bullet-riddled concrete structure in a seedy strip of Saigon—tomorrow.

Only now, and suddenly, they would have to wait longer than expected. They could hear the helicopter come in for a fast landing, could see the tension in how everything quickly, quietly stopped, then started moving at twice, three times, the pace. A table cleared, "Move aside," shouted at them, they suddenly feeling new, small.

Then the dust-caked man with the bloody mess in his arms stumbled in. His head leaned over something, so at first they could only see the man's dust-oranged green-metal helmet, but then flopping beige and black paws and legs became visible. The dog appeared almost delicate, with folded wrists, and wrapped in the dirty, sinewed arms of the handler. The sleeves of his uniform were torn away, his pants thick and heavy, boots crusted with mud. His rifle formed a neat diagonal line across his back, hard-edged metal against all this mush of hot, dirty uniform and man and dog. Their vision of a combat-weary soldier, only now no Vic Morrow tough guy, but a sobbing, yelling oversized boy, begging, Help me, help me.

They could see the dog was already dead. Everybody could see that. Even the handler knew it, but he wanted it changed. The handler thought, *I could be wrong, the dog could be in shock. They could do something, if I'm fast enough, brave enough, loud enough.* But he feared the spirit had already slipped away, even before the chopper had dipped into the smoky drifts at the clearing and lifted them out.

The vet tech--not John Carter, who watched dumbfounded, terrified, but the seasoned, expectant, collected vet tech--put his hands onto the handlers' arms and softly eased them open so he could take the dog from him. They laid him on the table and pulled their curtain with the snap, snapping motion. They would see if there was anything they could do.

The handler looked over the men with wild eyes. They saw his shoulder patch showing "41st Infantry Platoon Scout Dog."

"A dead spot," he shouted to their gaping faces. "It was a dead spot in the jungle on the trail. No air moving in it. He lost the scent. They knew it." He paced in a small circle-- "They were watching us. We were onto them. We nearly had them. Smokey was taking us to them. But the dead spot and we lost them for a minute. They opened up on us." He blinked and didn't see any of them, but kept talking, his hands hitting the blood-soaked front of his shirt. "When we were down the incline, they opened up. I could see the AK-47. Thirty meters away. Aimed straight at my heart. Smokey jumped up into the air. I swear to God. The bullet was for me. He took it for me. I know it. Right in front of it."

He looked again at them, then at his bloody hands.

"The round knocked him into me, knocked me over. I just held him to me, I couldn't do anything. I didn't shoot. Somebody shot the Dink. I couldn't do nothing. I was just holding him." And then the crying again, bawling open-mouthed, unashamed, then into his hands, then wiping his face with the dirty, orange hands, and back again. Finally, a giant, shuddering sigh, and folding himself into a chair, still with tears coming, but no means to deal with them, he slumped next to them.

The vet emerged and told the handler the dog had been shot through the heart, had died instantly, no pain, no fear, just death.

"We autopsy every dog. You want to wait and see the heart?"

The vet was used to these guys. They just couldn't believe the dog was really dead until they could see the death with their own eyes, and touch it. He sat in silence and waited, and at last the vet came out holding the purple-red heart. It was larger than Rusty had expected it to be, and they could all see it, could see the hole through it, could see that the bullet had gone in one side of the heart and out again through the other, and that the dog had been relieved of his life this way. The heart that pumped the blood, that gave the dog a life, now faced them, removed from the body and useless, lifeless. The spirit had evaporated. The mass of blood and heart and fur and scenting genius was now cut out of the man, too, and the man silently held onto his agony. The others in the room could feel it in the silence, and some of them, not thinking, closed their hands as if over a leash, or as if grabbing onto the thick, double-textured fur at the back of the dog's neck. That the handler was overreacting,

64

that it was the death only of a dog and not of a man, never crossed their minds.

---

Notes

Khe Sahn: Herr, pp. 86-166; Specter, pp. 117-41.

Vietnam-era mascots: Clark, p. 157.

Civil war mascots: Seguin.

Veterinary information: Clark.

Captain Robert Stecker, an American advisor in Vietnam, headed the program to form the first scout dog platoon with ARVN handlers in 1962. His biggest complaint in this task was that the dogs were as big—or in some cases bigger—than the handlers.

Major Pat Patterson, "First Dogs to 'Nam," *Dogman,* Articles section.

Suzi, Paul Morgan's mascot: Morgan.

First Vietnam dog death: *Dogman,* vol. 1, no. 1(March 94), p. 2.

Captions

p. 51: Members of the 47th IPSD heading to Vietnam, May 1968.

p. 52: Arrival at Bien Hoa Airbase.

p 54: Daryl Hubble.

# Sally

*Army Engineer (to 47th handler Tom Corsello): How much time you got left?*
*Corsello: Eleven months.*
*Engineer: Do people live that long?*

Rusty Allen, unpublished memoir

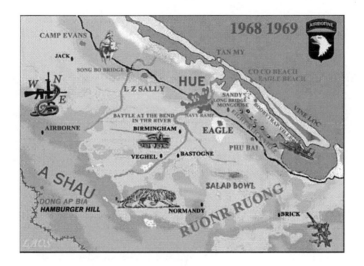

The 47th spent a month at Bien Hoa, mostly waiting. There were not the proper facilities for practicing their dog handling skills, leaving the men anxious and the dogs restless. Instead the men refreshed their own jungle warfare training, this time at the perimeters of the real thing. Early in July, the order to move north finally came, and they would leave greater Saigon behind them.

They flew to Phu Bai, north of Danang, and from there--loaded into trucks with all their weaponry, supplies, and the dogs in crates--they trundled up Highway 1 toward Landing Zone Sally. They passed through Hue, with its fortressed citadel modeled after Mandarin palaces of China, the stronghold of Buddhist monks and intellectuals. Piles of shredded structures were what remained of the ancient imperial palace and temples and once exquisitely landscaped parks.

They bobbed across an Army engineers' pontoon bridge, the only remaining way to leave the city, over the Perfume River, the Song Huong, and rattled onto a two-lane dirt road, still Highway 1, that was leading them to their new home.

LZ Sally was nestled along a bend in the Song Bo river on the edges of the Annamite mountains. This section of mountains had become a funnel for southbound NVA troops. Among the poorest and most sparsely populated areas of the country, it served as home to the Montagnard tribes, an indigenous people whose village and cave-dwelling culture was primitive, but whose sure knowledge of the land was unsurpassed. Americans worked to befriend the Montagnards for their expertise of the terrain.

Other denizens of the Annamites included elephants, tigers, panthers, boar, deer, monkeys, tapirs, bears, birds of numerous tropical varieties, raccoons, squirrels, rhinos, and crocodiles, not to mention the lizards, leeches, mosquitoes, spiders, and fire ants. Snakes included air gliders, pythons (twelve feet and beyond), vipers, cobras, kraits, rat snakes, wolf snakes, copperheads and various others. One company located in the area had a nearby cobra patch, and men were jokingly promised a three-day pass if they could successfully catch one.

Their east side held a gentler, though still threatening, land--sandy lowlands that traipsed a few miles toward the China Sea interlaced with rice paddies, fields of tall grasses, and woody patches; plenty of the snakes, ticks, and other creatures, among the mines and enemy personnel, were there too.

As they drove along, they could watch these pairings of landscapes and see the villages of bamboo huts with their coconut-leaf roofs and around them milling pigs, dogs, and chickens. Occasional lone shacks of patched together, castoff military supplies also sprouted along the sides of the road. Children rode silently astride slow-moving water buffaloes wading into the sparkling, watery rice fields, just like the pictures they'd seen at home in *National Geographic* or *Life* or *Time*. Men and women wore the dull black pajamas and woven circle hats they'd also seen, as near-naked children chased chickens with sticks. And then all this Edenic imagery would break with the sky-piercing of firearms, coming out of nowhere, tightening their insides, quickening their heartbeat, and then stop again, and return to Eden.

Despite the forward movement of the truck, the heat soared well over 110 degrees and the men felt every bit of it. Their feet, their legs, their faces, their hair inside their helmets, all wept streams of perspiration. Vietnam has four seasons that consist of two alternating climates-- heat with humidity, and monsoons with heat. It could also become cold at night, with heavy, bone-chilling mists smothering their attempts at sleep. Now they were still in the high heat of summer. Early fall, a few weeks off, would bring in the next rainy season. Air flows from south to north for the summer monsoon, bringing warm, heavy air from the Indian Ocean, and dumping it mainly on the south side of the mountains. For winter's monsoon season, the pattern is reversed and what was previously "rainy" in the northern areas becomes, after a dry season, perpetually saturated with water. This was a good place for growing things--rice and mosquitoes especially. The slap of men going after mosquitoes would ring in their ears for years.

"We're coming up on the camp soon," one of the escort troops announced to anyone.

The wide sky with its wisps of feathery, transparent clouds seemed everywhere. John Carter squinted, then

put his hand up to shade his eyes, as he spotted a red blot oozing into the air above the probable site. He watched as it spread across the surrounding sky and hovered there. *The camp's been bombed,* he thought. *We'll all have to go home now.* Still looking, he asked, "What's that up there?"

The guard chuckled and shifted his M-16 to a more comfortable angle under his arm.

No one wanted to seem stupid, so they didn't say anything more. They only stared. *We'll get the joke soon. It's all a big joke, and we're going to die in it.*

The trucks chugged up the incline to Sally's sawed-off hilltop. They drove through the gates and past the VIP landing pad, where the absurdly cockeyed statistics of the brigade's current operation, posted on an enormous board, blurred by: Total Enemy Killed and Captured—2140, Total US Killed—27.

They drove on to the center of the camp, which was a circle, half a mile in diameter. The camp was bisected by the landing strip; helicopters and light spotter planes buzzed like insects onto, then out from that line, spewing as they did gusts laden with the red, irony dirt that blanketed the entire camp, dirt that gathered and coughed its way into the sky, forming the red balloon over the camp.

The bulldozers of the Army engineers had left no tree or even clump of bushes to absorb the dust or shelter a man or a dog from the sun. The ground was like concrete. And the 47th IPSD was assigned the unoccupied patch of dirt connected to the airstrip. There was no running water or electricity, no tent or latrine. Dismal as the place seemed, the handlers were still unaware that to the average infantryman struggling out in the field, this was paradise. They would soon set up tents, with a cot for each man, and there were several mess halls across the base, so they'd be going where they liked the food and the company best, where actual hot meals could be found-- "three hots and a cot," the infantrymen called these reprieves from tinned rations and sweat-soaked, poncho-wrapped nights. But were the handlers to smile in appreciation of this, their teeth would be instantly coated with the red dirt. When you blinked, there was dust in the corners of your eyes.

"The dogs will suffocate," one handler said. They were all having trouble breathing.

******

The 47th was given a few weeks to settle in. Lieutenant Stockdale and Wahl worked out the system of the board with the rotation list of dog-man teams. No one had called them for a mission yet. Instead, the men, griping at what their specialized training had come to, had been passing the days filling sandbags to build a bunker and fortifications for their tents (no floors yet) and creating the dogs' accommodations.

Other dog units would soon envy the 47th's eventual set up. The men built wood platforms for the crates, so that they could be raised a few feet to avoid the streams of rain that would come soon, and to catch the elusive night breeze now. The dogs quickly figured out that the platform box itself provided a shady refuge during the day. They could lie under their raised houses. They were chained to stakes and allowed about ten by ten feet of open space. The men dutifully filled sandbags to surround the dog houses at first, but these made their sleeping areas even more stifling, so they were removed.

They walked, fed, and groomed their dogs daily, and there was training practice also. It was not a matter of organized classes anymore, though. A few nights of mortar attacks, the constant swirl of aircraft, the pained faces of returning troops made reminders to train unnecessary. Learning everything you could about your dog, working at making him happy, up, healthy, strong, and your own right arm mattered more than anything else as they awaited the summons from the infantry units.

Wahl had tucked Flexible, the mixed-breed puppy

they'd come across at Bien Hoa, into the plane and onto the truck for the journey to LZ Sally.

Rusty had a crackling, alive energy, but the routine work details the men were now assigned left him agitated and frustrated. He figured out ways around them and preferred to spend his time teaching Sig tricks. Roll over, shake, play dead, stand up like a rearing horse--all became activities to sharpen Sig, amuse himself, and impress the other handlers. Rusty had no doubt who had the best dog in the unit, probably in all the military.

As part of his job as squad leader, Otis kept his eye on Rusty. Otis had been a star football player in high school, recruited by colleges, and offered a full, four-year scholarship to Benedict College, also in Georgia. But in his junior year, Otis was sidelined with a knee injury. He lost his scholarship and became eligible for the draft, knee injury notwithstanding. Smart, athletic, experienced, Otis moved up quickly in training. His team skills served him well as a squad leader, and the men easily respected him.

He'd already come down on Rusty for his habitual teasing of Pearce.

"Leave off, Allen," he'd reprimanded him. "We're family here."

And now Otis was on Rusty about filling the

sandbags.

"I got it all taken care of, Otis," Rusty said.

"Well, I don't see any wall going up, Allen. We got to sandbag the bunker."

Mercer was passing by. Otis glanced his way, and nodded to him.

"Oh, it's okay, Otis. We've taken care of all that, right, Mercer?"

Mercer stopped and put his hands on his hips. He looked at the ground waiting for Rusty to annoy him.

"How's that?"

"Yea, we got Gooks doing it for us, a penny a bag," Rusty laughed. He turned to leave. "I'm going to walk Sig some."

"Christ, Allen, stop saying that," Mercer shouted after him.

"Easy, Chris," said Otis.

"He's always going on about 'Gooks' this, 'Gooks' that. It pisses me off."

"It's no big deal. Don't sweat it." Rusty was gone.

"We shouldn't even be here and he acts like he's doing them some big fucking favor."

"So. We're getting into that again."

"I never wanted to be here in the first place. I shouldn't be here."

"You used to be so quiet. Why're you shooting off at the mouth like this now? You're going to get yourself in trouble, you know that. Now settle down."

"I'll be quiet. Real quiet. I'm leaving. I'm going to go." He hesitated, then lowered his voice. "I'm taking off for the jungle."

Oh, Lord.

Mercer wasn't in Johnson's squad, but Otis somehow attracted those needing to unload. Mercer burned to  share his thoughts, his plan, with someone, so he could hear it out loud. Otis would listen to him.

Maybe the heat was getting to Mercer. Otis knew the kid was even less accustomed to this sort of life than the others. Tennis at the country club, maybe that was how Mercer worked up a sweat back home, but not like this. Otis had seen him in his tent, listening to classical music on his tape player, reading books, meditating, while the other guys played cards together. And he'd started spouting off from the anti-war articles he'd been reading in recent weeks.

Otis led him into his tent. He drew back the green mosquito netting that surrounded his cot. It kept some mosquitoes out, but stifled any movement of air, so you had to choose, slap mosquitoes or be sweat-glued to your mattress. He sat and offered Mercer the folding chair Wahl had managed to finagle from another unit for him.

So what was this talk of running off? To Otis, the tag of deserter was unthinkable. He hadn't wanted to go to Vietnam either, but here he was. He believed he represented his country now, that his country needed him, so he must rise to the occasion, offer it up for the team. He also knew Mercer was becoming an irritant within the unit. At Bien Hoa, it was rumored that Stockdale tried to have him transferred to another unit.

There were no takers. The integrity of the unit was everything to Otis, so he talked to Mercer.

Otis could talk. And the hours of gentle repetition, steadiness, and warmth Chris drew from Otis seemed to settle him. He cooled him down enough to hold on. Unit integrity was not that important to Mercer, but Otis was able to convince him of the folly of thinking he could survive the jungle, and of the certainty that recovery, if he wasn't already dead, would mean life in prison. He convinced Mercer of the sense of these realities. You had to get along, he explained. You had to adapt.

The dogs, too, were having to adapt. The weeks of quarantine were supposed to give them a chance to adjust to the pounding heat and thick air. German shepherds are intended as the all-terrain dog. Their soft, dense undercoat is the insulating layer--keeping the body heat in--with the outer coat of longer, harsher hair serving as a protective layer. In this hot climate, the undercoat shed out after about two weeks, leaving the dogs with a lighter, tropical coat and the slimmer outlines familiar from their photographs. In fact, though, the heat was devastating the dogs.

When dogs were first brought to Vietnam to be used by the South Vietnamese Army, trainers quickly discovered the effects of working dogs in 110 to 115 Fahrenheit temperatures. In one incident, thirteen dogs being worked by ARNV handlers fell in one day, by noon. Training was subsequently scheduled to avoid the midday hours from ten to two.

The canine first aid that the handlers learned at Fort Benning included recognition of heatstroke symptoms--rapid, shallow breathing, excessive panting, and rapid heartbeat, which could then advance to vomiting, tremors, and finally collapse. Dogs affected by heatstroke could go into shock, and were vulnerable to organ failure and swelling of the brain. When normal canine temperatures of between 101 and 102.5 degrees fahrenheit soared suddenly, to as high as 109.5, the dog could usually be saved by swift action--moving him to a shaded area, cooling him down with a water or ice bath, and sometimes administering  tranquilizers. Once a dog had survived heatstroke, though, he became more susceptible to it. If the body temperature rose above 109.5, the dogs normally suffered seizures and then death, regardless of the speed, efficiency, or method of treatment. Those who did  survive that temperature had no mind left, and were euthanized out of mercy.

In that climate, the dogs were nearly always struggling with the heat. The men had taken care to work the dogs in gradually increasing periods to review their training, bringing them outside the perimeter in groups for practice scouting missions.

They walked in small groups outside the barbed wire, not going after the enemy, but suddenly with their buffer zone of relative security lifted away, tiny noises taking on greater meaning. Though outwardly they shrugged it off, inside they twitched a little, or maybe more than a little.

On one occasion early on, they hadn't been out long, maybe twenty minutes, trotting slowly on a sandy trail, dry, scrubby plants scratching against their pants like long fingernails, when Daryl Hubble noticed his large dog, Trooper, walking in slow motion, mouth open, tongue hanging out, gasping for air. As Hubble watched, Trooper's legs wobbled, then crumbled beneath him, and he toppled helplessly onto his side. Hubble scooped him up and tried to right him, but again he collapsed. The men looked at one another as Daryl gathered Trooper into his arms, rushing back into camp. Trooper was taken to John Carter. His temperature had risen beyond 107 degrees.

Carter put the dog immediately through the cooling routine--pulling him to a spot of shade under a tent flap and dousing him with buckets of water, including the veterinary refrigerator's entire supply of ice cubes. The others watched in silence. Carter massaged the wet fur to dampen the skin, to try to revive the dog. He worked his fingers carefully, especially around the head, under the legs, in the belly.

Slowly blinking and with a moan, the dog eased back to consciousness, but glassy-eyed and confused, then anxious, attempting to lift his head. Daryl knelt beside Carter, hovering over Trooper, reaching around to soothe and stroke his dog.

This time they'd had good results, a close call, and Daryl felt the luck he'd had. It was the first direct threat to one of their own dogs. Daryl was shaken. The fear and brief panic he'd felt ran through all of the men who had witnessed the incident, including Carter.

"He'll be alright now," he reassured Daryl, "but this could be the beginning." He stood up from the dog, wiping his hands with a towel, lips squeezed together in thought. Other handlers stood nearby. Carter met their stares. Already he'd begun to develop the sure eye contact that doctors have, that gives confidence to worried patients and their families. Sparks of sunlight glinted off his glasses.

The heat was a larger problem than they'd expected, and so was the noise. There was a world of difference between simulated weapons fire in the woods of Georgia and the unpredictable slices through the night of incoming mortars, plus our own nightly outgoing harassment fire. The men felt it. But men are better than dogs at internalizing their fears, and their senses don't absorb the sounds as acutely either. The dogs might learn to endure the noises, but they still flinched at them. They would never cease to hear them or become inured to their effect. The shock of the noise itself--its volume and suddenness--not its consequence, since they couldn't know that, froze them in terror or sent them berserk. But they would have to learn to live with it. Their men knew that, knew that if they wanted to keep this dog, they must ease him and encourage him to accept and endure the noise as well as the heat.

They watched as Fred Severini's dog Tramp failed to adjust. He only grew worse with each pummeling of noise and flash and swoosh of artillery. They watched silently and exchanged nervous glances as Tramp destroyed his housing again and again, as Tramp's face grew pinched and his body thin.

These things made them focus hard. The men worked and trained, leading the dogs into this time, this place, this job. It wasn't all from love and devotion, of course. The men believed the dogs were their own best chance at survival too, that they needed the dog, this dog, to be with them, at all times during this episode in their lives. Their survival was interdependent, and so they nurtured the new canine soldiers as if they themselves knew what they were doing. They showed the dogs the way to lead them, as they'd done in Georgia. It was just more intense now.

And the dogs took care of them, too, even in these early times when they weren't yet going out on missions. They'd amble over together, in pairs, to the PX or across the base. A young man wanting to be cool, above the fear, the displacement, would be bolstered by this handsome specimen of a dog, strong, sharp, bold, who gave off some of that desired posture, that swagger of confidence, to the man holding the leash. Like kids on a playground, other soldiers would approach them, impressed, wanting to touch the dog, asking what they did with him, then reacting with amazed delight at the answers. The dogs introduced them, who they would be during this time and in this place, to the others there and those passing through. They *were* cool, and everyone wanted to pet the dog. They all wanted to forget where they really were and recall their own dog, tell about their dog, who was waiting for them at home, a friend and ready to play. They had that at home.

While far more than mascots to their handlers, the dogs did serve that purpose, too. Pearce could stroke Prince without embarrassment and still feel like a Man. He took pride in Prince's aggression toward anyone but himself. Pearce would act up, perform goofy stunts showing off for the guys, but in private he sought and found reassurance and comfort in the dog. Touching the dog's neck or head or running his hands along Prince's back would send the animal into paroxysms of joy. A touch to their dog could soothe any of the men and relieve the burdens on their minds--memories, mistakes, plans, the things they all thought about--but not only because the dog was soft, warm, and all theirs, but also because the dog knew nearly everything the man did about what to do *out there*. The dog would love the man as dogs do, but he would also lead him, stop him, show him what he the man would need to do. To keep that tucked away in your mind was healing. It blew a brief, cool, comforting breath of calm over them.

And so they kept the dogs with them nearly all the time, Rusty and Sig encouraging Pearce and Prince in the training lanes, Jim and Larry taking Pal and Fellow to splash in the Song Bo, Mercer traveling on daily routines around the base with Dusty. Regulations decreed that dogs must be staked out unless on missions or training, but they were more often found with their men.

Even when the dogs were staked out, the crate that was home to the dog had both the dog's and the handler's name stenciled onto it in bold, six-inch letters. When Otis passed by the dogs, or went over to them for any reason, he stood, cigarette in hand, hands on hips, and could see his own name there with Rolf's, and when anyone else passed by the dogs, they also saw "Rolf" and "Johnson" together. Each man could stand and experience a small surge of pride at this, their expansion of self.

The dogs had little notion of the future; the men wished to think as little of it as possible. This is why, though they knew their dog was only going to be theirs for a year, most chose to push away thoughts of that eventuality. Some did write to the higher reaches of the military or to their political representatives, seeking to keep their dogs permanently, but most thought more often of putting one day behind the next, not beyond that because the possibilities were un thinkable.

For this frame of mind, a dog was a good companion. If joy could be found in a present moment or in an ordinary, or even dismal circumstance, they would discover it. The future wasn't a worry when you let yourself into the dog's mind, because you were only there, in that moment, finding the best of it. Knowing transcendental meditation made Mercer one of the best prepared for this relationship. Focus on the dog, and the dog became the mantra. A box of stale cookies packed in popcorn from home, an afternoon nap, a belly rub for the dog--time experienced with the dog could be transporting. In the midst of these grand pleasures, little else mattered. When your back is against the wall, you can surrender happily to the dog's mindset.

Caring for the dogs also brought the men out of themselves. Regardless of how much he might not want to be there, Mercer still had Dusty, who needed his water, his exercise, his food, his training.

There was a mutual dependency between them, but the dog's needs were basic. What the men needed from the dogs was more complicated. The dogs did provide it to them, but did they do so knowingly, or because of qualities the men projected onto them? Did it matter?

******

The men, after working to set up their camp, a job they'd expected the Army engineers to handle, were also required to pull guard duty at one of the bunkers along the perimeters of the camp, something they hadn't expected or trained for. They executed this dutifully, including Jonathan Wahl, doing his share and bringing Flexible along, unschooled, but good company in the long hours. As the weeks wore on, men would sometimes doze off on guard duty, knowing their dog would take up the slack. When this came to light, the men were forbidden to bring the dogs on this detail.

It seemed to the members of the 47th that the commanders of the base assumed a cavalier attitude toward them, began to view the dog unit as a handy group of able-bodied men, available to take over some of the tedious details around the base. The dog men were specialists, though, and grew unwilling to take on chores that they felt were the bailiwick of infantrymen on base. Pearce was the lone exception. Anything he could do for the 101st, he did eagerly. The others felt they had enough to do keeping their unit right. Caring for and training the dogs was their primary responsibility. But it wasn't only a matter of not having sufficient time for basewide chores. It was a matter of pride, of status they believed they deserved, and they gathered themselves for a little good-natured rebellion. Larry Proper, though normally shy and deferential, joined with the others in the plan.

"You go on and do like I told you," the sergeant urged them, as they were set to report for another of these tedious, and in their opinion unwarranted, calls.

And when Larry and the others strolled into the mess tent, reporting as ordered at 0430 hours for KP, they held tight to the leashes that strained with the eager, salivating dogs.

The mess sergeant glared at them, hands quickly moving steel covers over the tubs of spongy scrapple and watery scrambled eggs.

"What're you doing with them mangy mutts in my tent," he thundered.

Then the men shuffled and gathered themselves, shrugging and nonchalant.

"We only work with our dogs," said Larry quietly. "We're not to be separated."

The disgusted sergeant waved them away. "And don't come back."

The victory dance ended quickly, though. The entire first squad was about to be called out on their first mission, an extended stay in a place that would forever define the word "hell hole" in their minds.

---

Notes

Animals in Vietnam highlands: Huynh, Clark, and various.

Snakes: Camden-Main. Gliding snake, also known as the Flying Snake, is *Chrysopelea ornata*, p. 71.

Viper patch: John Herschelman, email 1/9/02. Despite the offer, Herschelman continues, "I do not recall anyone ever getting a three-day pass for anything, much less for catching a cobra."

Rainy seasons: Weidenkopf, pp. 443-44.

Heatstroke: Clark, pp. 31, 147; AKC pp. 612, 672, Gerstensfeld, p. 471.

Captions

p. 70: LZ Sally.

p. 73: Jim Adams and Fritz.

p. 75: Otis Johnson and Roger Hermann.

p. 77: The Hubble twins, Daryl, left, with Trooper, and Bert, right, with Butch, received special permission to remain together throughout their tour.

# Mongoose

Firebase Mongoose was a scratch in the sandy lowlands southeast of LZ Sally and northeast of Hue. It rested inside the lacework of coastline and inlets that border the China Sea. The sand was bleached-bone white and sprinkled with sprouts of acid green grass that gave way to lush thickets of feathery bamboo, brushy clumps of trees, shrubs, and vines. Beyond a small canal lay a camp of South Vietnamese soldiers, ARVNs, and a tiny village, a few hundred meters outside the base. Farmers worked the surrounding rice paddies, while children fished from narrow wooden boats or looked after the water buffalo, and also scouted for the benefit of the Viet Cong, who permeated the area.

Mongoose provided backup support for platoons working in the surrounding areas outside Hue, especially the sprawling village known by its wide dimensions--the Eight-Klick Ville--where near-constant searches consistently produced enemy personnel, and where mines were consistently planted and replanted to undermine those searches. For those working the ville, or out on the trail, in the brush, or in a paddy, Mongoose was the place you radioed when the situation called for artillery support.

Mongoose served as a command base, the center point for the operating areas of a variety of units, as well as a drop-off site to resupply those working out in the field. It did not have a PX or a mess hall, hooches or showers. The men slept wrapped in plastic ponchos on muddy floors of dugout bunkers. In addition to the panoply of heavy artillery, varieties of launchers and explosives too cumbersome to drag out into the field, it had two miniscule helipads. Mongoose was a weapon waiting for targets. Noise was nearly constant: 105-mm canons fired relentlessly, as medevacs popped in and out.

Because of its location, security was always tenuous. The NVA seemed to know their movements almost as soon as they themselves did, and perimeter sweeps grew increasingly lethal: The surrounding terrain was seeded with mines and booby traps. The ARVNs were barely cooperative, and the loyalty of the village was always dubious. Looking for any advantage on the enemy's intimate knowledge of the place, the commander at Mongoose decided to try dogs, and the call went out to the 47th.

Since Mongoose had requested an entire squad, and for an extended period, Lieutenant Stockdale knew the squad leader would have to assume an unusual amount of responsibility. His men would have to look up to him, listen to him, obey him. He would have to command respect, but also tend to them as individuals. Instinctively, he turned to the first squad, and Otis Johnson, its leader.

Otis would bring his men, Rusty, Pearce, and the other squad members, to this place to be on hand for missions worked around the camp. Knowing he would likely require use of the dog teams repeatedly and over a period of at least weeks, the base commander at Mongoose believed the teams would be safer (and more accessible) if they remained at hand, instead of attempting frequent precarious and time-consuming insertions from Sally. For the men and dogs of the 47th, it meant isolation from their unit, as well as cramped, rugged living conditions that made Sally seem luxurious in comparison. Their assignment would continue for nearly two months, and three of the dog-man partnerships would dissolve by the end of it.

******

By the time Stockdale spoke to Otis and then Otis gave his squad the heads-up, Rusty was almost eager to get going, to do *something*. Pearce yahooed at the news. "Finally. We're going to see some action now."

"Leave off it, Pearce," Bagatta grunted, then helped him pack his rucksack. Bagatta's dog, Rebel, was one of the smartest, quickest dogs in the unit. Small, blond, with foxy features, Rebel had already made a deep impression on Bagatta, who himself was dark, heavy-featured, and stocky. Growing up in his Italian neighborhood in Brooklyn, Frank did not have a dog and had not given much  thought to pets. Rebel was, at first, a novelty. Like so many of the others, Frank found himself marveling at his dog's abilities and sense during training, and at his own connection to the animal.

Bagatta admired the dog's capabilities and his composure in the midst of any situation. He believed that the dog would see him through. Rebel's comportment during work and while at rest was both calm and alert, and encouraged Frank's own geniality. In fact, most of the other handlers also admired Rebel. Sig was the best known among the dogs, the big hotdog, performing tricks, as clever and brash as Rusty. Rebel's demeanor was cool and modest. He quietly aced all obstacles.

Pearce's dog, Prince, on the other hand, was developing a reputation for being among the least friendly of the dogs. Scout dogs frequently landed in brief scuffles, but other handlers began deliberately to avoid Prince when they walked around the base with their own dogs. And he wasn't the sort of dog who would buddy up to humans either. He'd sneak a nip at loose hands when he could. These were not negatives in Pearce's eyes. He took pride his dog's sometimes-surly attitude, maybe even encouraged it with juvenile teasing and his own awkwardness and apparent lack of tenderness.

Then Otis interrupted the packing with a tug on Bagatta's sleeve. Otis and Frank with their two dogs would leave now, ahead of the others, who would join them the next day. Otis trusted Rolf, and he trusted Frank and Rebel. If he were putting his men at risk, this was the safest bet. Frank was tough and good-humored, and they'd worked well together. Otis saw him as steady, not liable to flinch if things got heavy. By arriving early, Otis figured, they would get a sense of the mission overall, get to know their commanders, and learn what was expected of them. They would set things up, and have the situation in hand before the others arrived.

But when the Hueys came and took them away, and

with the others watching, stomachs suddenly fluttering, they never got the chance to discuss the mission generally or even their own first call-out specifically. The chopper took them straight to the field, and dropped them right into it.

*****

"Hey LT, listen." Otis was waving his large hands. "This just ain't the way to do a search."

"Can them dogs find mines, or not? I was told them dogs could find mines."

Otis looked away, hands now moved to his hips, mumbled, and let it trail off. On his first mission, and already things were not going as they'd been expected. He and Rolf were not leading the platoon down a trail as they'd always trained to do. Instead they were sweeping an area around the camp, and not from the point position. The men were spread out in a horizontal line, with about five meters between each one, and the dog team was simply one among them.

"They're supposed to *follow,*" Otis continued to no one, but by now the platoon was positioned into a broad fan shape. Frank and Rebel were with a second platoon in another nearby area.

And not only was the formation practically useless for the dog team, the environment was nothing like the marshy pine forests of the American south where they'd trained. It had poured rain through the previous night, and the place felt, looked, smelled, thought Otis, like steamed greens. The shock of the abundance and impenetrability of the grassy vegetation: *This is thick, thick, thick,* he kept thinking. Rolf hesitated before it. He would have to push through the green mass. The dog was distracted, too, by birds and other, unidentifiable twitches and screams and shrieks that called out all around him. The normally solid worker appeared on edge.

"Search, Rolf, search." But the tension in Otis's voice was easily read by the dog, and Rolf himself glanced back and forth at the new sensory distractions, his eyes skipping from ground to air to tree line, his ears cocked and nose probing. Both struggled to focus. And what was the point, anyway? What good could they do like this?

For several hours they pulled themselves through the dense wet grasses of abandoned and overgrown paddies, sodden earth springing and squirting under their feet. Then Otis and Rolf made their first contact with an alien force, not soldiers or mines or traps, but the tiny and silent *phylum Annelida*, the class of worms known as leeches.

Otis felt a slow trickle ease down his neck. He was hot, but this felt different from sweat, and instinctively putting his hand to it to check, found smears of blood and felt the lump. He started to pick at it, but a soldier, spotting him, stopped him.

"Don't pull it off, Johnson. Hold on till we break." Otis twisted his neck in frustration.

The front end of the leech has a small sucker and a pair, or a couple of pair, depending on the species, of eyes. Leeches breathe through the skin. Waiting in tree branches or bushes, or in streams and rivers, they lift their front end and drop onto a victim, attaching with the small front sucker and with a larger posterior sucker. They range in size from minute to about eight inches, but can stretch themselves out even longer. Three sets of jaws contain sharp teeth that make a Y-shaped incision. The saliva then excretes an anesthetizing substance that also dilates the blood vessels to increase blood flow and, further, prevents the blood from clotting. Hirudin, the anticoagulant obtained from certain leeches, can be used medically for humans.

When they rested, Otis found more creeping around his ankles. Checking Rolf, he discovered several on the dog, two or three attached to Rolf's groin and one inside his left nostril.

Of the approximately three hundred species of leeches, some live in fresh or sea water and feed on the blood of fishes, amphibians, birds, and mammals, or eat snails, insect larvae, and worms. Land-dwelling leeches feed exclusively on the blood of mammals, and in the area, it was not uncommon for domestic animals to die from suffocation when leeches blocked breathing passages.

While it is possible to become infested with leeches internally, by swallowing water, or just bathing in it, which could lead to anemia, for the soldiers in Southeast Asia, the principal threat was of external infection, especially if the insect was torn off, and bits of it remained in the flesh. Some soldiers carried bottles of iodine with their gear. Scratches, mosquito bites, or any number of means of exposure to what swirled around the atmosphere there could ignite dangerous infection. It became second nature to splash iodine on any kind of intrusion into the skin. Flies were always there to conduct their business, too. They quickly attended any opportunity to feed and leave behind bacterial calling cards.

When they rested briefly, the soldier walked over and examined the dark, wet blob. He pulled out his bug repellent and doused the creature. It writhed.

"Here go." He lifted it off gingerly and rolled it in his hand a second so Otis could see it. Then he tossed it back into the green behind them.

"What about my dog? I can't pour bug juice up his nose." Otis lit a cigarette and squatted down next to Rolf.

"Use that thing," said the guy, "burn the sucker. Just don't pull it out till it's all the way dead."

Otis's hands, one steadying Rolf's jaw, one positioning the cigarette just so to sear the life out of the leech, trembled as he moved in on it, and Rolf bobbed and jerked his head in resistance. The whiff of roasted leech. It constricted, and Otis, with large fingers slipping over it, caught its skin with a fingernail. The intruder was extracted. A series of relieved and hearty sneezes from Rolf, and they gathered up and moved on. After this initiation, and in the face of the other, more extreme dangers they were heading into, this act became a simple reflex. They would automatically check for such things, and deal with them, without much thought, as they cropped up. Leeches were creepy and sneaky, and they wanted to suck your blood, and they were an annoying little part of the life they were now living.

And they did head into bigger things. Between the leeches and flies, the screaming birds, and the rain-slaked grasses now dried again by the sun, the worst that could happen did happen, and someone stepped directly onto a poised boobytrap. It had sat there through the day, waited for this soldier in the earth, creating with his footstep the explosion of free-flying fragments of steel and plastic and all matter of other materials that also hurt those standing beside the one who actually touched the mine nearly as badly as the primary wounded. It happened time after time throughout a long, grim afternoon. By six o'clock five men were wounded and the helicopter had swept in to collect them. They had exchanged fire once—for five sudden, mad, and excruciatingly endless minutes—and killed three NVA.

They continued like this for three days, and when they returned to Mongoose, safely it turned out for Otis and Rolf, Frank and Rebel were there telling the same story. The two of them attributed their survival to luck, not skill. Otis was furious.

By then they could see what Mongoose was, and the rest of the squad had gotten there as well.

"Hey, Otis!" Pearce was lunging toward him, a big wave and a smile for him. "Otis, this is a cool firebase, huh?"

"A shithole is more like it," he snapped, and stalked past him. He questioned the others in the squad about the conditions of the bunker, where they'd been idling for two nights, and went to the command tent.

"What is the point of calling up a dog team if you're going to use them on a sweep line? And how do you expect my men to work when they're living in that mudhole in the ground? The dogs are tied up in plain view, the rats are dancing the cancan all night, we're getting bled dry by mosquitoes, we've got no hot food, nothing but C-rats—"

"Make the best of it," was all he got in reply.

Otis returned to the others and faced the accommodations.

"Rusty. I don't believe even you could stand up straight in that tiny bunker." The skies opened up to rain. It fell in soft sheets through yellow-tinted air. "Let's make it tighter." The rain intensified. They scrounged plastic bags and stuffed them wherever they could to get the bunker to leak a little less. They dragged over some extra sandbags.

"I went in first, Otis," Pearce offered.

"Yea," Rusty smiled, "and there was only about thirty rats there ahead of you."

In a bunker built for two, the six would sleep together like spoons, though there wasn't much sleeping. Too much rat action, too much slick mud under them, too many mosquitoes, too much artillery thunder. And meanwhile the dogs were staked out, in the open, above the bunker. The wet earth vibrated, on-off-on-off, through the night.

"My mission sucked," Frank said that night, waiting for sleep. "But the grunts were good to me. It was like they wanted to take care of me."

"They treated me real good," agreed Otis. "Pearce, you get to sleep. Stop fidgeting."

******

Over the following days, Otis grew more confident of the squad's abilities. He accompanied each team as it worked in the field for the first time, then let the proven teams go out alone or with another green team. It was then, as Otis was easing into some semblance of a plan and a routine, that he was approached by the base commander with a special request.

"You understand this is sort of unofficial."

At that time there were still a number of Marines operating in the area, mostly assisting with security. Every square foot in and around the Eight-Klick Ville required checking every twenty-four hours, and the bridges over the canal near Mongoose needed constant surveillance. Four Marines had gone to the bridge the previous day, accompanied by an equal number of ARVNs. They had not reported in that morning, as would have been customary.

"They're not even a mile down," he said. "I don't like it. Think you've got a team to find where they've got to?"

Okay, thought Otis, this we can do.

"I'm thinking there could be mines down there."

"We can handle it."

Otis returned to the squad.

"McMahon, we're up." He and Rolf would go, and he would take Joe and Alex, his dog. It would be a straightforward mission, and brief.

Each dog team led a platoon along separate trails, and though it was less than half a mile to the bridge, it took nearly an hour to reach it while searching for mines.

As soon as they grew close to it, Rolf gave a major personnel alert, only instead of a neat sit with pricked ears, Rolf went berserk. Otis could barely control the surging animal. The dog's eyes appeared wild, his body jerking and jumping. Otis had witnessed unusual alerts in Rolf, but nothing like this.

Otis came across them in the sandy dip under the bridge, and along the cloudy water's edge was another experience for which no training could have prepared him. In the first few seconds, he didn't recognize what was before him. He was hit first with the smell, and then the vision of the black frenzy of a million flies. They were everywhere, coating and skidding across the surface, spinning and jumping like a black breeze. Instinctively he waved his hands in front of his face, jerking the dog, and being jerked in return. He penetrated each spasm of despair — the hysterical barking of the dog, the putrid air, the whine of the flies--to find what they'd been looking for. The Marines lay positioned under the bridge, their throats sliced open from ear to ear. By 11 a.m. they were already bloated and exuding the fetid, gamy stench of the opened body and spilled human blood. The ARVNs, whether accomplices or bystanders, had fled into the countryside.

When the dog ceased barking long enough for him to speak, the lieutenant asked Otis to remove himself and his dog from the scene, and they stumbled to the other side of the road.

******

On the next day, they went out again.

"God, I am ready for this," announced Pearce.

But Otis said, "You'd crap in you pants if you got shot at, little boy" He handed Pearce a canteen and started filling another. "Now quiet down."

Pearce screwed on the top and spoke to himself: "I'm going out."

Otis looked to Rusty. "How're you doing?"

"I'm sweating like a pregnant nun on her way to confession."

The three teams were to head out now for several days, checking the village and surrounding lands, searching out the mines they were certain were planted throughout the area. Three platoons, three dog-man teams. It was time to see if Pearce could handle himself. Otis would be out there, too, as would Rusty and Sig. Pearce would be well buffered this way.

At the helipad they ducked the tornado of the blades and scrambled into the Hueys. Sig bounced skyward, dragging Rusty up and slamming his handler into the metal sides of the opening, which forced the steel pot over his eyes. Rusty quickly knocked it back, glancing around to see if the indignity had been noticed. The pilot stared straight ahead, smiling.

Up into the chopper after their dogs, one team after the next to join the three platoons already camped on the way to the ville. The hit of cool air, Sig slumps to the floor, eyes closed in bliss. They all heave a breath in, and the chopper drops lightly down through the air, stomachs left behind. It tapped the ground, and then lifted up again.

"Sorry guys, it's too hot here. I can't stay."

The dog teams soared out as the chopper climbed, and was gone. Otis landed on the knee that had given him so much trouble in college. He limped to cover with the others.

*****

When they had all gathered up into their separate units, and the LT of Rusty's platoon began setting up the mission, broad sweeps, Rusty argued back, as Otis had done earlier, that they were wasting the dogs' skills this way. He met the same resistance.

"I don't expect a dog handler to tell me how to run a

sweep, okay?" Rusty felt his greenness and backed off. But first they had to get there. And for that, Rusty would walk point down a trail that ran through the countryside that enclosed the village.

"I'll lead you *to* the ville alright anyway," he said. The lieutenant didn't know it was his first mission.

*****

The trail was hot and sandy, with scads of thick, tick-heavy grass sprouting like fright wigs alongside and across the trail. Rusty tried not to think too hard, tried to put himself into the place where all he thought of was  the sand in front of him, his leash, his dog. Watching the dog, and getting into Sig's rhythm, he began to experience the synchronicity he'd only touched on before. It had never felt so complete. He began to breathe easier, in time with Sig, it seemed. They began to move as a single gesture through the land, and all the others behind them became part of the wake of their energy. They were always aware of the others behind them, but they flowed together, cutting through space, aware of absolutely everything.

Then the dog magic began to happen in earnest. The ears went up, the body froze, paws sliding into the sand, and Rusty could feel the electricity of the dog shoot into him, the flow broken, by something there.

Rusty gives the signal and the line halts, in silence. They can't see anything. The lieutenant orders them on even though Rusty insists there's some kind of booby trap hidden up ahead in the sand. He knows, just knows, without having prearranged or trained this particular signal, because he felt it from him. Why else would Sig slide his paws into the sand that way? There is something there.

But being ordered, he urges Sig on. Sig moves forward tentatively, then gingerly steps off the trail, skirting an invisible area, and Rusty knows just where it is now. He stops and kneels down, Sig waits, and Rusty fingers the sand in that area. Everybody behind him has stopped again. He brushes gently over a small lump he has felt and there it is, a ball of C4 explosive, with a detonator attached, just enough to take off a foot.

He's terrified at the discovery, but he doesn't care because the satisfaction of this accomplishment pushes that fear away, or maybe just adds extra adrenaline to it. He looks back. Everybody has seen it; and everybody knows just exactly what it is, and knows why somebody's foot or leg or worse wasn't lost to it. They move away, backing up step by step in their own footsteps, and they detonate it.

Then they keep going. The sand fries Sig's pads, but he's too keen, too determined and excited and full of game to care. The sun glares off the sand into a shocking sort of light. Another hour goes by and Sig alerts again — this time Rusty can see them, three traps, and he signals to the others. But just then Sig finds something else. He's up and wiggling and lunging into the air, and Rusty knows again without thinking about it, Sig makes it plenty clear, *Forget the poppers, there's somebody there.*

Rusty signals the others down, and they, complete believers now, confer and decide to move around the poppers, marking them for later detonation, to find who's there up ahead. Then Rusty, holding onto a wild-eyed, twisting, but still, thank God, silent Sig with one hand, and hoisting up his M-16 with the other, calls, "There he goes!"

He sees him between the branches and vines, waiting for them, but can't shoot because big Sig is practically dragging him ahead. Sig wants to catch him himself, forgets himself for a moment, and the others begin firing. They rush toward the NVA soldier, but Rusty stops them. There are more traps ahead, and they will find them. They reach the ville an hour later.

Then the frustration of being put on the sweep line, fanned across the diameter of a section of the ville, uselessly placed as one among the regular infantrymen. And the other platoons were near them, and now working in the same fashion.

They trudged through long, snagging grasses and scumbly patches with bare lumps of dusty earth. The dog handlers, not seeing each other, separated by trees, but knowing they were also out there sweeping, felt the deflation of the intense, singular purposefulness they'd just experienced. There was an anxiety in feeling one among many, two feet randomly stepping forward, the dogs jumpier now, too much distraction for them to focus forward.

Rusty heard it—*slam pop crush*—and flinched. Not close, it had to be from one of the other platoons. Radios working, static voices shouting clipped words, back and forth, and a glance over from the radio guy to Rusty, and Rusty sinking inside. "Some people from second platoon's hit. One's a dog handler." And Rusty moved helplessly on, hating not knowing all of it, only knowing it was Otis. Medevacs, movement, and then walking forward and continuing many more hours, until the day finally ended. All that time, not knowing or speaking about Otis, only hoping.

That evening, when the company came together for the night, he searched out the second platoon's medic to find out the rest.

"I don't know exactly how bad it is," said the medic, "but Johnson won't be playing any more football." Otis had been hit with fragments flying out from a booby trap when another guy in the line alongside him stepped on it. Two from that platoon were killed during the day's operation, and several others were wounded. "And the dog got totally weird. Went crazy and wouldn't let me at him. They said to shoot him." The medic stirred his tin of ham and lima beans and began eating.

"So then what?" asked Rusty.

"So then they just distracted him, and somebody grabbed the leash and pulled him away off of Johnson." The medic continued eating. "They were ready to shoot him, though." But Rusty was thinking of Otis. He wanted to find Pearce now, to tell him. The medic called after him as he walked away.

"Hey Dogman," he said, still cramming the ham and beans in with the plastic fork, "he was conscious when they put him and the dog in the bird." They wouldn't know more for months. Otis was just gone.

*****

The next morning, same sun, same heat, no finds yet as they faced, then crossed a massive paddy. On the other side, the heat was so intense it burned Rusty's feet, even through the thick leather of his boots. And all the time he thought of the pads of Sig's paws, which must be sizzling with each touch of the trail, and of the dense coat smoldering around him.

Watching Sig, the dog seemed to sway as if in a breeze, which wasn't there, and then try to hop through it, hopping a little, then swaying, wobbling. Rusty watched, knowing they'd recently cracked open the last of the nine canteens for the day. Then Rusty knew to stop. He squatted down next to Sig, and called back to the lieutenant.

The LT orders the medevac, helping Rusty fumble aboard as Rusty lifts Sig, who is not able now to jump up on his own. Rusty's steel pot slides forward, wet with sweat, until he pushes it out of his eyes. He settles back into the chopper, not noticing the pilot at all now, only stroking the dog, heading back to Sally. He pours the last canteen over Sig's head, working it around his ears and toward the skin, as much as he can.

---

Notes

ARVN: Army of the Republic of Vietnam (then South Vietnam).

Mongoose was washed away by Hurricane Bess in September 1968.

---

Captions

p. 88: Otis Johnson.

p. 89: Frank Bagata with Rusty's dog, Sig.

p. 96: Joe McMahon and Alex.

p. 100: Rusty Allen.

# Pal

Days after squad one left for Mongoose, Jim Powrzanas headed into the field for his first mission. The call in for a team , Wahl glances at the board and rises. His head appears through the tent flaps. Pal lifts his eyes toward Wahl.

"Powrzanas, you're up." Jim's eyes over to Proper. The nod back, no words. Puts the cards down, walks to his cot, and starts packing, tries to stop thinking, like he was getting ready for work at the airport, just putting things in order, a regular workday. Pulling out and lining up his stuff, then Pal's, running through the checklist. Pal emerging from under Jim's cot, stretching out and arching his back; yawns, shakes himself thoroughly. Big smile and the saber tail swinging. He knows. He spots the harness now and he's wrapping himself between Jim's legs, flexing right and left in happiness. Jim sorts out the legs and the harness and puts everything in the right place, Pal forgetting he ever knew the word "heel," straining the length of the leash. Jim, reassured, sighs low and slips on his rucksack, finally pats his steel pot in place. The others watch him jostle the back weight until it rests right and then walk across and over to the strip to wait for the Huey. They go back to what they were doing.

The two figures stand on the red-dirt strip for two hours, then the hum of the chopper grows louder, then breaks into droning throbs, and a sudden, flattening air blast, shouting, the lurch up, the lift and the coolness. See you in a few days, everybody. A pang of homesickness for Sally surprises him.

He had all the innocence of his boyhood on his face, but it was a mask. Fear had frozen the mask in place, numbed his emotions, and shut his mind away from any thoughts except those that enabled him to continue following through — picking out the required equipment, preparing his dog, waiting for the helicopter, getting his briefing, walking to the point position, feeling the platoon behind him. He kept a plain expression always in the field, from this first mission. He nodded and led Pal to the spot at the head of the line, and then went about his business deliberately. Of the team of two, it was Pal who let his emotions spill all over the place, tail whopping and swinging, mouth open in a toothy, head-raised dog-grin. He looked like a dark, heavy-set sled dog right before the big race.

As he gathered himself into the pace, he began to force a rhythm through his head, so that he was only walking, walking in the woods. That was essentially what they were doing, just as he'd done all his youth in the pine forests of Pleasant Grove, Alabama, outside Birmingham. This is what Jim was saying to himself, or trying to. How many times had he done this in his lifetime? Walking along sandy-soil trails, with their iron-hued soft edges, cutting through the woods with friends on the way to school, or to the place of his great passion, the baseball field. The town was home to only about a thousand people, but you were always with groups. More often than not they were cousins, or cousins of cousins. You were surrounded by countryside, but you never felt alone or isolated.

Now he felt the full strength of aloneness. The men chugged along behind him, boots moving silent as slippers now, all of them with their heavy packs like his, and all of them behind him, but not including him. They were connected to one another by their shared experiences in-country. What bound these men, unrelated by blood, would endure at least the length of their lives. They were lifelines, each to the other behind or in front of him. Together they would see death and life and bodies turned inside out; together they would commit what they once considered mortal sins. They were the people they would possibly die with or for. They were glued together.

Within the military's training philosophy, unit integrity--caring deeply for the welfare of the others in one's unit—is paramount. It is good strategy because it motivates the men to kill others for one another when conceptual national goals can seem vague and distant, at best. For many in this particular war, there was no other reason to fight. Part of the harsh treatment they all receive in basic training is designed to bring them together. One man may be singled out in a class by the training sergeant to become the object of his derision, the "goat." The particularly derogatory treatment he receives keeps the others unified, to avoid his predicament, and it offers them a relative sense of successful achievement.

As their experience deepens with actual combat and the deprivations of everyday existence that accompany it, individual differences become insignificant as the men unite to survive, relying on one another with a depth that remains a unique bond for life. This day, a terse, crackled radio call later, Jim and Pal were thrust among them.

The dog team had no connection yet to these people, only to each other. Jim and Pal were alone together. For some in the platoon, having the team boosted their confidence, for others they were intruders. Jim knew that, but he also knew he must not think of it. He must focus himself entirely into the dog, forming the unit of We Two, forging ahead into their job.

Then they're in the middle of the woods, Pal sparking along the trail, now trotting, then, and mostly, stepping, drinking in every sound and smell and ion-charged airborne message that wraps around this, their little world, quick sniffs, then moves on, all business in every stop, somehow knowing he was running the show yet also completely oblivious to everything but Jim and the air and earth. Knowing that the quieter you are, the more you can hear, he tunes out the guys behind and easily becomes one with it.

Here in the lowlands undergrowth scribbled green and brown up from the white patches of sand, creeping over the dunes down into the trails that led into forests, through villages. Tall, spindly trees waved their downy foliage over them. Other trees were mere skeletons, their green life stripped off in bombings or mortars' fire.

Jim tried to lean back, not in ease, but just in calm, only Pal tugged the leash; the dog, his partner, was strong, urgent, restless, happy, ready. And so, shifting out of thoughts of Alabama summers, of walks along boyhood trails, of paper mills' putrid mists, he came back to the feathery brush around him. And Pal tugged.

Pal understood he had a job, and he loved his work. And by having a life, with purpose and relationships, Pal became an individual of specified character. Jimmy had taken this animal, and by working with him had shaped him. He had taken Pal's latent character and encouraged it into full bloom.

And Pal had done something too. While Jim held onto the leash, an energy flowed between them, so that as Pal grew out of Jim, he also transferred to Jim some qualities of being an animal. Pal embodied physical power and a comprehension of the natural world, and he fed that back through the leash to Jim, the startling sensory quickness that brought with it an understanding of what was There. While they worked, this electric pulse of nature came into Jim's hand and coursed through his body until Jim, the interpreter for all this instant harvesting of information, understood it, felt it too. Together, as one, they walked at the head of the line.

Nathaniel Tripp, an infantry platoon leader elsewhere in Vietnam, describes his attempt to understand walking point in his memoir *FatherSoldierSon*:

> This is how it works. You really have to concentrate, clear your head of all other thoughts. You have to become part of the jungle. Part of the secret is how you move, but if your head is in the right place your body will follow, and you move as though doing Tai Chi, as though you are mist in the jungle. You move your body, then you freeze. You

move your eyes. You move your head side to side. You listen. This is what hunters try to do, but it is very different when people are hunting you. If there is moisture, raindrops or dew, you look at every leaf to see how the droplets run down. If some droplets are running differently, somebody was just there. You listen for what the jungle sounds like, listen if the jungle's heart skips a beat. If a leaf is bent, you look at the crease and see if it is turning yellow and think about how long it has been since somebody else was there....but there is more, which is harder to describe, which goes beyond what you see and hear and sometimes even smell. It is the part about going outside your own body, and seeing with the third eye. This is the part that is most important, and the most frightening, because it is the most powerful stuff on earth and if you use too much you go nuts. I understood this, but I never was all that good at it and found my position in the rear of the point squad vastly preferable.

As they walked along together, Pal became Jim's third eye. And if, while walking point, a human finds his senses aroused unbearably, almost to the breaking point, what must be the level of the dog's in the same position? Already they imbibe the signals of nature with a depth beyond our comprehension. When Pal put himself into that hyperfocus, his sensing abilities so much richer, his reception so much keener, tuning into things around him with an acuteness we will never know, smelling, hearing, seeing, tasting, simply feeling all the stimuli in a blanket, an almost-crushing load of sensory input, what could that be like? He could transport himself away from fear, hunger, or pain and into a land of awareness, beyond the physicality that is within our world of reason, and then he would tell Jim about it, read it to Jim. Pal became his sensory translator.

And so Jim also learned to extend his awareness even possibly beyond that of those infantrymen behind him. Only he could read Pal, as only Pal could read the land and every living thing that surrounded them. And in those times when they rested together, Jim could lay his hand on the harsh outer coat covering Pal's thick bones and muscles and absorb Pal's strength, energy, even his serenity, but now working, there was no peace within Pal and Jim, only awareness, a constant inhaling of life.

They continued on, taking the time as they required it, slowing the regular pace of the patrol. This was beginning to irritate the platoon leader toward the back of the line, irritating him even more when Jim stopped them all so he could put Pal in the water and let him rest. The LT grudgingly gave them the break while Jim cooled Pal down. But then they had to walk on again. The woods were thickening and night fell in closer. Pal slowed even more.

The word came quietly up from the rear, *Move it, Dog Man.* But Jim was somewhere else now. Pal was stopped, nose bobbing up and down, drawing up the air left and right and front, slowly moving that antenna nose across the world before them, twitching those radar ears. What he smelled went straight into him--people. Jim felt it too, and knelt, and one by one, all the men behind them knelt down and hoisted up their rifles to their shoulders, and limbered up their fingers ready to act. They stayed like that, as Jim swung his free hand, the other holding the leash and his rifle, across the landscape. And he waited.

The LT crept up, and Jim whispered to him that there were enemy personnel in these darkening woods. Somebody was there, and waiting for them. It was unsafe to proceed.

The LT was not pleased. They hadn't yet reached the point on the map where he wanted them to camp for their night. He glanced around and stood up.

"This mission calls for us to reach an abandoned ville six klicks up. We'll search it, and then strike it. That is the plan." The B-52s were already ordered up, so they would ultimately have to get at least a mile past that village.

"I'm telling you, sir, there's an ambush up there."

"Move it, keep going."

Jim also stood, though he knew the stupidity of it, and gathered himself to follow the order from the officer. They walked on twenty more yards. More alerts. More orders to move from the LT.

"Sir. I told you. There's personnel all around us."

"It's not that far, just keep going."

"But I'm telling you--"

"Listen, *Private*, go on."

Deeper into the nest they traveled, Jim now moving to the rear of the line, his job done, his piece said, and all the time his knowing the worst would happen anytime the Others were pleased for it to. They quietly set up their camp and ate cold rations, Pal too, but no flashlights, no fires, no talking. They lay on their sides in that darkness, and lying there in the blackness, the stillness noisy with its tiny sounds magnified by the quiet--the birds, the frogs, now quiet too, unusually so-- and then in that stillness it came.

First a whistle, a crack, and a slam, and the night sky blistered with white-red light, the light of noise that soaked up the night and then pulled it open with ringing, popping, and terror, which they were trapped deep inside. There was no place to go, because the NVA had had plenty of time to set them up, had been watching them, and only Pal and Jim—maybe even most of the men—had believed what the LT wouldn't. If only they'd sent up an advance team to search and scatter them, if only they'd listened to Jim. But all Jim could think was, *Why do these people hate me this much?*

He held onto Pal. And in this storm of rocket-propelled grenades bursting red and tracers racing at them green and voices of pain and fear and the staccato notes of automatic weapons ringing into them, relentless, unceasing, all of Pal's training left him. The dog twisted and barked wildly and lunged away from Jim, so that Jim had not only to guard his own life, but also preserve the dog's, to keep him from running away, from jumping in front of the artillery in or out. But he was also grabbing the dog from deep inside his own fear. He would be protecting the dog and keeping him alive and with him not entirely because he was worried about the dog, but because he was, in some part of himself, the same as the dog; they were connected, extensions of one another. As their searching energy had earlier, their fear flowed between them.

When it was over, ten minutes and a lifetime later, Jim found himself lying nearly on top of the dog to hold him there. Around them, three men from the platoon lay dead; nearly a dozen others were wounded.

The next morning, with the dead and the wounded lifted out, they were ready to return to the trail. Jim's head stretched forward, eyeing the dirt, then scanning up to the trees, seeing slender branches and twisty vine tendrils, but imagining snipers, claymores, leeches, monkeys, everything fecund and poised, the night before still throbbing through his head. He clicked the leash onto Pal's halter. But as he executed this ordinary, everyday act, automatic now, like pulling on socks before boots, he felt something, the tiny rush, the warm-water flow up from Pal, suddenly new and richer, more majestic, than he'd known before. The full source of Pal's energy went into his fingers and traveled up through his arms, spreading over him.

He smiled, knowing he understood something he'd never admit to. He had experienced terror last night, of the deepest, most primal sort. The fear had reared up before him, and he had felt every sinew of his own body electrified with it. He'd been drowning in fear, but he'd had one hand on his dog, one arm stretched out of the ocean of his fear to grab onto something else, to guard its life, the dog himself twitching and flailing, a toffee-colored embodiment of Jim's own emotions. The dog turned his head to Jim and opened his mouth in happy anticipation of a new day together. For Pal, last night was gone. Its moment was evaporated, though its traces would never disappear entirely. And once having encountered that moment together, nothing would be the same between them again. Wherever they went now, it was from last night.

Because of last night's fear, too, Jim knew he could now live inside the state of fear, that instead of being afraid, he'd be wary. Never again would he expect normal; he'd expect last night and move through days, not waiting for it, but just knowing it might be there. He would stay ready. Only in this way would he be ahead of Pal. And everything that Jim now knew to be true about

Pal—his silent knowledge of what was there, the vast, encompassing awareness that skipped over the trees or hiding places or other physical boundaries to go straight to what he sought—would remain with him forever also.

When he returned to Sally, he related to Lt. Stockdale, as he was supposed to, the alerts, and also the ignorance of the mission's LT about dogs and what they could know. He didn't say much about the firefight, except for the plain fact that it occurred. The details of it, and the feeling of it, really didn't have any bearing on the success of their mission; it wasn't something to go into. What mattered were the correct alerts. And maybe if he didn't describe it out loud to anyone, it wouldn't exist anymore.

The next time out, the walking at point seemed more sure. So when Pal froze and the hair on his neck lifted and he raised his head, Jim also froze, and died a little inside. Then he eased, just a quick breath, as Pal looked back at him, conveying in his back and legs and his eyes and face that it was something, but not a living thing.

It was rice, a lot of rice--400 pounds as it was later judged. And Jim, his heart beating under his tongue, calmly saying, "Check here", there's something.

Moving to the rear, as he was supposed to do, two or three others poked into the sandy mound until they found the rice.

Then later, at point again, Pal's ears popping forward, then turning eager to Jim, pointed out a bigger find, two concealed Viet Cong bunkers, containing 75 recently used beds. There were also dozens of weapons hidden there. The bunkers would soon be destroyed; the weapons sent in. A shy smile escaped from Jim's placid face. Pal understood that they'd found the prize and won the game.

On another mission shortly thereafter, working up from Pal and through Jimmy, they found booby traps, including at least two with 250-pound bombs attached. But on that day, two men from the platoon strayed off the path, did not walk where Pal walked, and stepped on more traps. They were taken away by a medevac helicopter.

By the time he returned from the third or fourth of these early missions, Jim believed he'd fallen into the perfect team. He said nothing to the others about this. They could think what they liked about their own dogs. Jim knew. Nothing in this world could be one hundred percent sure, but he knew Pal was worthy of as much confidence as was sane to assume. Because of their union, he believed he could face what was ahead.

Soon another mission. Suddenly they were pulling many in August. Up in the Huey, to the landing zone, meet the guys, start the line, move along the trail, all as before. Hours slid by, and they crossed a paddy dike, the sun picking away at them, glinting off Pal's coat between branches and on open trail, Pal panting, now heavily, and canteens emptying as the day continued. As they headed out of another abandoned village, Jim stopped at the well, its green-brown water swimming with invisible life, and lifted his helmet off of his head and dipped it in. The men wouldn't drink it; they still had canteens left, and they knew its bitter taste, sometimes adding Kool-Aide to it to cover its taste and the taste of the water purification tablet. But Pal's thirst was urgent, and Jim knew the dangers of not letting the dog have enough water. So he dipped the steel pot into the well, and extended it to Pal, to ease that thirst. Then they continued on until they reached the stream where Jim could stop and wet down Pal entirely. He had begun to seem worn out, as the dogs generally did after working several days in the field.

There were no more alerts that day. The enemy had dispersed, had been driven out by artillery, and moved on. The platoon reached a clearing and the end of this leg of the mission. Jim and Pal loaded themselves onto the helicopter for LZ Sally, Jim staring ahead, absently stroking Pal as he lay, tired now, unsmiling, on his side on the floor of the helicopter.

Jim noticed Pal's fatigue, remembering the heat, the wet air, the briars scratching on his pads, the sheer weight of all they'd seen and all he'd done recently. They both needed rest.

He took Pal to the vet tent and left him with Carter while he went to brief Lt. Stockdale on the mission. But within minutes Wahl, quiet and quick, pushed into the tent, trying not to look panicked, and cut into what Jim was saying.

"Carter says you'd better get over quick. Something's wrong."

Jim blanked; he forgot what he'd been saying to Stockdale. Stan had been listening, taking notes for the After Action report. His eyes widened, "Go ahead and go," he nodded, and laid down his pen.

Jim strode into the tent. Pal was lying on a table, and John had his hands on Pal's neck and side. The dog was coughing, then retching and twisting. John cradled the phone against his shoulder, "I'm talking to Phu Bai," to Jim, then back into the phone, "I did the Ringer's. There's no change. He's starting convulsions." Then to Jim,

"Powrzanas, what happened here do you think?"

Pal threw his head up and down. It clanged onto the table and his legs began trembling harder.

"I didn't think he overheated."

"It's not heatstroke. Did he get into anything?" And speaking rapidly to the vet on the phone, "Okay, I'm injecting atrophine."

Jim hovered next to Carter, who was holding onto Pal's shaking, then jerking body.

"No, nothing. Ephenephrine? Yea, okay." Carter moved fast while Jim felt his uselessness, a frantic impotence. Then Carter was loading Pal into Jim's arms.

"We're going to Phu Bai," Carter jumping behind the wheel of the jeep, turning to watch Jim clamber in with Pal, grinding the gears neatly, and then patching out in a burst of red-clay dust.

Jim wrapped his arms around Pal, to stop the seizures, to squeeze the pain and bewilderment out of him, to hold his life close and almost into himself. Jim pushed thinking out of his head, tried only to connect somehow to Pal, to reach him on the plane he had so recently discovered and entered into.

But it was too late. With a sigh and a shudder, the dog's muscles relaxed in unison; it was over, and Jim was telling John to stop the jeep, and Jim then knowing Pal was gone, had soared right out of that ruffled fur and bony teeth and red gums and curled tail and hyper-tightness. The piece of himself that could say, Everything will be all right, was no longer there.

And, expressionless, Jim laid his face into Pal's fur neck, pulled him closer, then eased his grip. He held him comfortably, easily. He turned his face, still resting on the dog's shining coat, to the side, and stared past the red dust into nothingness. Abandoning his reserve at last, he allowed his features to constrict and his body to cave, and he sobbed like a little boy whose heart had broken, big painful sobs through heavy stinging tears, as Pal sailed away.

Later, Carter asked him about the water, if he had let Pal drink from the local water, and Jim remembered the small well. John said it had likely been the water in that well. The water had probably been poisoned by the VC, which they sometimes did when they retreated from a ville, knowing the Americans were not far behind. Pal would be autopsied and they'd know for sure then.

Jim could feel the thread they'd formed between them, man and dog. It was as fragile as air, but as strong as a force of nature. It would entwine them forever, and it was now a pain so heavy he wished he'd never known the dog at all. At that moment he swore he would never allow himself to care that much for another living thing.

---

Notes

Building unit integrity: Fussell, also Hedges.

Firefight: Since after action reports are not yet available for the 47th IPSD July-November 1968, the casualty numbers are from memory. Powrzanas recalls 3 killed, with approximately 10 wounded; Rusty Allen recalls 4 killed.

---

Captions

p. 107: Larry Proper (left) and Jim Powrzanas.

p. 108: Jim Powrzanas and Pal.

p. 121: Jim Powrzanas and Pal.

# Ears

The so-called Eight-Klick Ville was more a series of minute, scattered villages than a single particular village. It meandered up and around, roughly shaped like a U that wrapped around a large group of watery rice fields. Houses dotted the trail that laced in and out, tracing through the letter shape. The area was supposed to have

been evacuated, but every few houses along the way held the remainders of the families who had lived there — grandparents, children, a few mothers. Able-bodied family members had gone to fight (against the Americans), so that those still in residence, while sometimes outwardly friendly, were always to be carefully watched. Those who had gone to war were not far away. They streamed in and out under cover of darkness, constantly laying, changing, and re-laying traps and ambushes for the Americans and South Vietnamese troops who monitored the village.

Of those still there, the children frequently made friends with soldiers on their patrols in and out of the villages. Kids would greet soldiers, do small favors, and beg treats. But even children could not be trusted entirely. Once when Cliff Searcy, an infantry soldier, looked to greet a familiar child friend, the child appeared reluctant to approach him. The boy stood in the trail, tense, arms squeezed to his sides. When Cliff called out  to him, he shook his head, lips pinched together. Cliff approached closer, and suspicions aroused, put his hand on the boy's upper arm. He felt a large bulge at the back of his sleeve, as the boy's body stiffened, eyes anxious, fearful, ashamed. Cliff reached inside the boy's shirt, grabbed a live grenade, and tossed it into the trees, where it exploded harmlessly. The boy had been made into a human booby trap.

A dog would have alerted to that grenade straight off, and the units that patrolled the Eight-Klick Ville had grown aware of the benefits of the dog-man teams there. The randomness of the booby traps, and the endless imagination of the placement, kept the men on edge, and the handlers provided a sense of slight improvement in their odds of survival. Patrols were constant, in and out of the ville, so if the pressure could be ameliorated, even a shade or two, it was a relief of sorts. It did not relax the situation, but it provided an alternative possibility for some increased security. Plus the dogs were fun to have around.

The guys on this patrol were glad of the dog. They were less pleased with the handler. He had an arrogance that had not engendered much friendship over the past few days. It was Mercer, and they could not mistake the aloofness with which he regarded them.

For his part, as he stepped along the dirt in the trail, watching Dusty, noting also the clumps of broken tall grasses, Mercer contemplated the irony of the Buddhist presence in his current location. Maybe this entire experience was an illusion.

Whether in the field or back at Sally, he continued to meditate every morning, in the face of teasing from the others. Eventually they grew tired of the joke, and left him alone. Still he found no inner peace. Even when he slept, the agitation never left him.

And here they were again, he and Dusty, pushing through the heat, now moving in another useless horizontal formation. Pointless, he thought, meaning both without a point man and dog, and without any purpose also. They crossed a into treeless area, so the sun was directly on them, and sweat soaked through his clothes and made Mercer's steel pot slip forward and feel just a little more uncomfortable than normal. He jiggled Dusty's leash and the dog glanced back at him. Dusty offered a weak dog-smile, a flash of inner lip and teeth, before turning back again and continuing. They'd been out three days, working full days, with sleep-deprived nights.

Regardless of their conditions, the dog was not to blame for his misery in any way. Dusty was exempt from everything Mercer held against everyone else. The dog had charmed him entirely. This was true for most handlers after they'd spent time with their dogs. No matter the handler, his attitude or personality or reason for being there, the dog was set apart from the rest of what was there. Each dog was his handler's link to something within himself, part protection, part comfort; strength and tenderness at once; unwavering dedication that you couldn't help returning.

Mercer appeared hard, or just bored, but he was as afraid as any of them, now silently moving a step at a time, half-crouched, waiting, moving in measured steps, eyes ahead, then on the dog, up, around, and on the dog again. He also lived in the constant state of awareness and readiness. Once, back at Sally, when he fell asleep with a flashlight on his chest, he woke screaming into the night, throwing the metal object across his tent because he believed it to be a rat. The others never let him forget that. And on his first mission, dropped into the mountain trails along the fringes of the Ashau Valley, he had thought tracer bullets, with their green zip-zip, careening movements, were surrounding them, when they were only fireflies, silently going about their business.

But this time there was no confusing real for imagined threats. Dusty had already found one small booby trap today, tucked into the earth. And Mercer knew the odds of finding more—they were there. Knowing what happened at Mongoose, and working now in the same lethal formation, Mercer realized how vulnerable they all were to the hidden traps. His clothes stuck to him, but he barely registered the heat anymore. Watching ahead was more important.

Dusty began moving more slowly now, and Mercer looked between the dog's ears. He was not alerting. He did not sit or move around a plot of the grassy field. Instead, he wobbled a little in his forward step. Mercer thought, Do I ask for a break to give some water to the dog? How long do I wait? Dusty had never hesitated before. The heat had not seemed to diminish his interest in the search. But now it occurred to Mercer that the dog was not himself. He glanced toward the platoon leader, in the middle dip of the wide, loopy line. He saw Dusty cross his front legs and wobble again as he struggled ahead. He whispered to the man next to him to pass along a request for a rest and a drink for his dog. But the lieutenant brushed away the question.

Mercer could see a few half-naked trees ahead that might provide some small bit of shade for the dog. If they reached the area soon, that could ease the dog's temperature. He looked again toward the lieutenant, but their eyes did not meet.

And then Dusty, with a heavy panting heaving of breath, buckled under the weight of the heat. His legs jerked up in crimped convulsions. He began shaking.

"My dog!" Mercer cried out now, forgetting and not caring about the dangers. Dusty's eyes were open, full of fear, confused. Mercer grabbed the dog into his arms and ran to the thin group of almost-trees, with their sprinkling of shade. He opened his canteen and poured its remains onto the dog's head and along his side, massaging him, quietly urging him to be alright. But he had waited too long. The collapsed dog could not be revived.

Stunned at the silent suddenness of it, he stroked the dog and stared at Dusty's face, squatting. Maybe he would revive now. He waited. Perhaps if there had been a stream handy to lay him into, it might have made a difference.

The others began gathering quietly around him, with "Can I help?"s and "Want my canteen?"s and "Man, he looks bad." Mercer stiffened and felt his isolation, the severing of this part of himself. He hated the men behind him for it.

Then the medic was kneeling beside him, checking the pulse, the eyes, the ears, feeling the heat in the dog's groin, and then giving Mercer the look that told him there was no hope, no life left. The medic stroked the side of the dog, "Sorry." And backed off. A few sat down around the trees. The LT came up and told them to Get their Sorry Asses Moving Again. He looked at Mercer, and, not knowing what the handler was supposed to do, looked away and kept walking.

Dusty was perfectly relaxed now, his long bony, collie face completely composed in the narrow blade of a German shepherd body. A light breeze ruffled the silky coat and lifted its blond outer hairs for a second. And Mercer just stared, now sitting fully on the ground, ankles crossed. His hands still held the leash, and they rested in his lap. His mind was blank, but he was trying to force something into it, a What to do Next idea. He lowered his head over his lap and onto the dog. The LT had sent one of the men back to him, "Come on."

Mercer would not leave the dog there. He slung the body across his shoulders and arranged it on top of the heavy rucksack, still loaded with two more days worth of food and water for the dog. He would not toss that out right now either. The soldier gave Mercer a look of incredulity, but said nothing, and they continued on and joined the others.

Mercer's head and neck began to ache from the

weight of the dog, and the awkwardness of his position. Soon the body would begin to stiffen. In this environment, death settled in so much faster. He carried it until their rest break.

"I'm going to bury him now."

"No way. No time. Sorry, kid, just leave it here."

There was the terrible fear of being discovered by VC; there was the anger at the officer telling him he could not bury his dog; there was his beautiful dog. He would not leave the body there.

"There is no way I am calling in a medevac for a dead dog. Now let go of it. We're moving. You can't use your weapon with that on your shoulder."

But he carried him some more, the coat tickling the outer edges of his face, the body pressing against his neck until he felt his head would burst from the pressure and from the extra heat of the 80-pound fur coat now draped around his neck and shoulders, until the weight of it seemed stupid and useless, and the LT ordered him to put the dog down on the grass and leave it there.

"You're a gun now, and we need every one. I can't put my guys at risk because you want to bring that dog with you." It was painful to leave a dead body behind, and the lieutenant understood that while leaving the dog was not anywhere the same as leaving a man's body behind, still it felt wrong to the handlers, even this one. But it was wasteful enough to lose a live man trying to retrieve human bodies. To gamble now with men so that the dog's body could come back was unthinkable. Mercer understood that too.

He slid the dog to the ground, and as he did it, he was remembering with disgust what they'd been told in training about what to do if your dog died in the field and you had to leave the body there: If you couldn't bring your dog back, you were supposed to cut off his ear--the one where his number was tattooed--and bring it to the vet tech. The vet tech could record it as an official death then. Mercer couldn't see doing that.

Nobody wanted to say anything to the stone-faced handler, who stared straight ahead as the dog lay stretched out at his feet.

He focused on a tall, far away, spindly tree. With no breeze at all, it was leaning to the right, a wisp of a tree weighted over by its own few lush leaves. The medic approached him. He put his hand on Mercer's shoulder as he squatted next to him.

"Want me to do it?"

Mercer kept the tree in his eyes. "Don't touch him."

The medic gave Mercer's shoulder a quick pat and stood up. He dropped his scalpels, in the slim black leather kit, onto the dirt next to Mercer, and went back to the other men.

Mercer ran both hands through his hair--cropped, dense chestnut waves. Piercing eyes squinted into the distance from his square, impassive face; his body was squarish too, fit and tight. He reached for the kit.

He opened it and slid out one of the knives. All this time, this short and reluctant military career, he'd dreaded finding himself in the position of killing another person, imagining that it would be a North Vietnamese man or woman, and instead he found himself here, in this awkwardness, hovering over his dog, contemplating cutting into his dog. But he would think in another direction. His eyes would glide up the thin column of tree, and he would hear the slip of breeze begin to whisper.

Mercer had spent time in the ancient, dark-leaved, big-bear forests of northern California. They were cool and blue-lit, not these scratchy, strung-out grass patches. Hours and years of time gave a boy a knowledge of the natural elements, one that grew into a palpable friendship. Focus back into his forest, float into it. Mercer could do this, and completely.

Rusty, Jim, Larry, and the others, but especially those who'd known him since NCO school, had seen it. They'd witnessed Mercer disappear into his trance more than once, at Sally when he had night watch, but most memorably at NCO school when the training officers had harassed Mercer, as they'd harassed them all, and Mercer was ordered into a prone position, the "Dying Cockroach," for some minor perceived infraction.

They'd all experienced that humiliation, on your back, arms and legs stuck straight up into the air, frozen there until the sergeant fancied releasing you. But they all remembered that time Mercer had gone into the Cockroach, his own way, fading into his trance and then refusing to come out of it until, screaming and near-apoplectic, the training sergeant ordered an ambulance. Only then did Mercer relax his limbs, and roll onto his side.

With his superior education and undisguised air of condescension, Mercer was not well liked by the training staff. But Mercer, like his pioneer, Scottish ancestors before him, didn't look for people to like him particularly. And it was for this, ultimately, that he failed to graduate from NCO school, drifted into the Casual

Company, and was selected by Stan Stockdale to be a dog handler.

Stockdale had been right, too, to believe Mercer suitable for the job of dog handler. Mercer did love his dog, clicked into him, worked as one with him. Mercer didn't fawn over Dusty outwardly. Others noticed that Mercer and Dusty worked well as a team, but otherwise their relationship was unremarkable. That was the image Mercer wished to project. And, Dusty, with his own reserved demeanor, kept his end of the deal as well.

Dogs have an eerie ability to penetrate the emotional armor of people who appear outwardly cold. They can soften the hardest souls among us. What is it that animals do that melts the human heart? They witness our character without embarrassment; they comfort with complete humility. When the dog and human accept one another, there is mutual satisfaction in each other's company. A dog can speak without words to someone whom humans find impenetrable. Maybe it is that simple fact—the opportunity to love deeply and be loved in return without having to admit or even acknowledge it out loud--that moves the immovable.

Dusty's gentle soul had touched Mercer. The dog was long and lithe. His tail curled the wrong way around, that is, up, and his face was also long, and angular. Not the perfect form for a German shepherd dog by a long shot, but he carried himself with a delicate grace. He was a sable color mixed with blond, especially light around the face, and with burnished accents on his ears and haunches and across the top of his tail. His attenuated canine beauty made a striking contrast with Mercer's own muscularity.

Mercer had spotted the Collie in him, not just because that would make him a little bit Scottish, but because of his longer, fine-boned legs and also because there was a sweetness to the dog. Theirs was an unspoken, utterly dependable closeness, mutually understood. When he sat, Dusty's legs splayed outward like a fan. Mercer never mentioned it to anyone, but he found this gangly pose amusingly goofy, even dear.

Now Mercer shifted his gaze to examine Dusty's ear. He kneeled over the body and balled a fist. He slid the fist inside the ear's smooth, cooling skin, stroking the fur outside with his thumb as if it were the tawny, velvet-gloved hand of a slender girl. His heart sank with sadness, but this was quickly pushed aside by a mushrooming of anger and frustration

"Just leave him," one from the squad, not unkindly, called softly. They were all sorry the dog died; they'd like having him there. They'd seen a lot of men die, but this felt different, less routine, more personal, and recalled to them their own pets waiting at home for them. Mercer hadn't said much to them over the days they'd been together, but the dog had been nice company, friendly. They liked dogs. He watched Mercer for a minute, then turned away.

Mercer said nothing. It's just an ear, he was trying to think. They'll get what they asked for.

They wanted it in order to prove the dog wasn't just lost or taken by the enemy. VC or NVA soldiers reportedly got a bounty payment if they brought back a tattooed ear of an American scout dog.

But it was Dusty's ear, graceful, long, svelte, like the dog's body, like the dog's long nose. It was a radar that swiveled and rotated and twitched, gathering information, that housed, at various times, fleas, mites, even leeches. How can I separate it from its host, holding onto it like it was a lucky rabbit's foot, and leave the rest of him, disfigured? How can I do to him what others have done to dead soldiers here--when they have found dead VC or NVA and cut off their ears to taunt the enemy and keep as grisly souvenirs?

Soldiers on both sides of the war did this routinely. Americans, Australians, Vietnamese; infantry, Rangers, commandos. One soldier reportedly had a whole bag of them, "like pieces of dried fruit"; one put an ear in a letter to his girlfriend (who never wrote back); one strung a necklace of them and called them "love beads." It's a primal gesture that has occurred after lynchings, too, here in the U.S.

You hardly notice an ear most of the time, but when it's removed from the body it belongs to, that disfigurement becomes horrific, as if something ephemeral about the person's very being has been denied. He is degraded and dehumanized. Ancient Greek literature is filled with the human angst, and the angering of the gods, with defilement of the dead. The body, whole, has a sacred quality, because we believe it contains a spirit. Cutting off a portion of it violates the sanctity of the person's identity and compromises the validity of their life. The completely vulnerable body has been preyed upon, and for fun, a joke. It is as if the spirit has been divided from itself, and we instinctively draw away from the gesture, and from the thing that has been removed from its host. And when you become the one doing the cutting, then you find you have lost some of your humanity as well.

A bitter anguish overwhelmed him and in the end allowed him to conquer his abhorrence for the deed. It was all so absurd that he must complete the absurdity.

He concentrated on the whorls in the coat at the base of the ear, the brown, cream, yellow mingling of individual hairs that produced the glow of mink-golden color, and he pushed the blade through them and under and around them and, without breathing in or out, closed his eyes and folded it into a small plastic bag, which he shoved into his hip pocket.

Then he carried Dusty's body over to some bushes and nestled him into the leaves. He sat next to him, pulling grasses, cutting his hands, and laying them over the dog, until he was well covered. Mercer would work as an infantryman now, until an appropriate time came to remove him from the field. He was dogless now, except for the ear.

---

Notes

Civilian massacre in Hue: Sometimes cited as a My Lai in reverse (and much larger). *Vietnam*, Feb 2001.

Cliff Searcy: An infantryman with the second platoon, C Company, 1/501, 2nd Bde., 101st Div.

Ears: Herr, 34, 199; and many other sources (Caputo, Tripp, etc.).

Captions

p. 124: Prince 74X1, Dan Tupper's scout dog, 1970-71.

# Dog Medic

Construction for LZ Sally began in February 1968, six months before the 47th's arrival, and it was still evolving that summer. Because it was to be home for an entire brigade, it was a sizeable base, able to house the artillery, light aviation, and other support units—including the scout dog unit--of the infantry operations. Infantry units would be mostly out in the field, returning only occasionally, and for short periods, to the home base between missions.

When they first got there, the dog handlers slept on cots in simple, dirt-floored tents. Showers for the unit were not installed until mid-August, when visiting Seabees voluntarily built them—a tin-roofed shack of three stalls, with a water tank on top heated by the sun-- as a return favor for drinking water that one of the  handlers had given them earlier. As summer wore on, army engineers built raised wood floors and added wood frames to their tents—improving chances of sleep during hot and, especially, rainy nights. And by then, scrounging pieces of discarded scrap wood and metal and screen, John Carter had fashioned a primitive but serviceable vet hooch of his own.

Inside, Carter had organized his metal cabinets to hold the dogs' food supplies and the standard medicines that John would use—alcohol, saline and antibacterial solutions, vaccinations, flea and tick deterrents, worm pills, and other drugs, including tetracycline and penicillin, which sometimes aided soldiers returning from local brothels—an examining table, and his desk. Just outside, a rubber bladder that had been used to deliver fresh water to the area was cut in half and became the dogs' bathtub, used for monthly dipping for parasites.

While at Sally, the dogs' day began with a visit from their handlers. Each would clean up his dog's area, rake it, and often visit with him, playing for a while, or brushing him. If the handler noticed anything wrong with the dog--cut pad, ear infection, runny stools, lethargy, limping--he would bring the dog to John to be checked. If not, the dog and handler normally spent several hours training.

Carter held regular "office hours" throughout the morning. Aside from checking for routine problems, including stitching up wounds resulting from occasional dog fights, John would vaccinate, draw blood for heartworm exams, collect fecal samples to check for worms, clean the dogs' teeth, and dip them for parasites, all on a regular, ongoing schedule. He looked after the pet or mascot dogs also. The army didn't object: mascot pets were considered good for morale. Carter himself  always smiled to see Flexi prance in, her feather-tail dancing behind her. Later, he might drive to Phu Bai to look at the blood and fecal samples under the microscopes in the larger, better-equipped veterinary facility there, as well as observe the vet surgeons, and even sometimes bring back special supplies—steaks, or beer and sodas. (Veterinarians, in their alternate role as food inspectors, had access to "gourmet" supplies.) Sometimes others would go with him, including a dog or two to unofficially guard the truck of supplies.

Among his most critical jobs was determining the fitness of dogs to go out in the field--they were always checked by him before leaving for missions. John wanted to be fair to the dog and the man, yet he also did not want to toy with fate, either. If he pulled a dog (and therefore his handler) out of the regular rotation for a minor health concern, he would in essence be sending another handler and dog into the field--ahead of schedule. Life-shattering events during missions were so random that John liked to adhere to the prescribed listing as strictly as possible. Then the luck of the draw, and not his own intervention, would determine fates. On the other hand, if he sent an unfit dog team out, he was endangering them and the entire unit they would support.

Carter also saw the dogs when the teams returned, checking for heatstroke, parasites, and injuries, and recommending further treatment in Phu Bai, if required. Here John would also sometimes glean the sort of information from the men that was later buried away, worries, traumas, or a proud recounting of the dog's achievements. He knew how each dog fit with his handler, and occasionally saw things that troubled him in that relationship. He had noticed one handler's cavalier attitude toward his dog, Jake, and his generally loutish demeanor, and on the afternoon that the handler arrived with the animal injured, he felt uneasy.

"I could have set this. Why'd you go to Phu Bai first?" He checked along the dog's head and moved his hands across his body and under his belly, quickly. He didn't trust Jake much, either.

"It was closer. I thought it was an emergency."

"He stepped in a hole?" Carter touched the splint and bandages covering the dog's left hind leg and realigning the broken shaft of the thick tibia bone.

The handler's hands rested on his hips, elbows akimbo, jaws slowly moving a wad chewing gum. Carter could be such a tight-ass. What did he know about being in the field?

"Just out of nowhere. We were walking along."

"Out of nowhere."

"Damnedest thing."

"On the trail?" Carter stood bent over, scratching a few notes on the dog's medical card, then dropping it into the four-by-six-inch, olive green metal box on his desk. He looked up at the handler.

"No, we were making camp, you know,…"

"And what?"

"And then he just, you know, starts with the crying out and limping. I look down and there's the leg hanging down. I think he twisted it stepping in a hole or something."

He left the dog with Carter and went to give Jonathan Wahl his After Action report. This was a qualified handler, and Jake performed well as a scout dog. But Carter knew the man had a temper. He doubted that the man had intentionally hurt the dog to get out of going into the field. More likely Jake had received the blunt end of his handler's frustration, just as an exhausted soldier might have flung a canteen against a tree, or kicked a steel pot lying in his path, knowing them to be lifesaving instruments, and for that moment, not caring. He did not believe that the dog had hurt himself in this instance. But speculation was not his job. He listed the leg as broken in the field, and left it at that.

Outright, deliberate abuse of the dogs was rare. Beside the fact that most of the men truly cared for their dogs, the initial purchase plus food, accommodations, and training of the dogs made them a $5,000 piece of equipment by the time they arrived in Vietnam. Unnecessary harshness toward the dogs was unacceptable. But neither were the dogs coddled or spoiled. They were expected to perform and were disciplined when they didn't, since lives depended on them. That normally meant a sharp reprimand; disapproval by voice or, at most, a choke-chain correction was normally enough to elicit the desired behavior. The occasional kick or shove, however, was not unheard of.

Nor were the dogs themselves perfect tin angels. They wouldn't be there if they weren't very good at their jobs; the long, vigilant weeding process continued throughout the dogs' service, eliminating them from the program if they could not perform to standard. The dog Tramp, the one who repeatedly destroyed his own dog house in fright during artillery exchanges, was one of several slated to be sent to the dog training detachment in Bien Hoa for evaluation. But even among the best of them, there were good days and bad, times when their senses were up for the game, and times when they broke loose and fought, refused commands out of fatigue or unexpected conditions, overlooked critical dangers in the field, or went berserk under fire. Despite their training and human interaction, some just never overcame negative feelings about humans or other dogs. The handlers understood all of these things about their dogs. Yet not one of them would wish to be without their dog on the trail. Not one would have preferred to be regular infantry.

As dog handlers, they were normally out in the field no more than four or five days. Working much longer than that would strain the dogs' abilities, and thus endanger human lives. So the men would return to Sally to rest their dogs, normally spending as many days in the base camp as they'd spent out, before getting another assignment. The infantrymen of the units they supported spent weeks, sometimes months, in the field, with no showers, decent meals, or shelter. One infantry unit serving the area during the same time period spent eighty-eight consecutive nights out, another nearly one hundred. Typically, for their safety, when out in the field units moved to a new position each night, digging in and setting up a night defensive perimeter, night after night, not knowing with complete certainty what surrounded them. Dog handlers never lived that way.

And there was more, not always outwardly acknowledged by the handlers. Like regular infantry, the handlers had one another, and these bonds also would survive time and individual differences. But they had something beyond human camaraderie, something that added bales of strength to the inner, private reaches of the self: their dog became both receptacle and purveyor of direct love, constant and uncomplicated. As their time in the war stretched out, as they faced down fear and pain and death together, the bond only grew in its intensity.

The handlers did a lot of communicating to their dogs with their voices — coaxing, talking, teasing,

sometimes shouting. And the dogs used voices too. They sometimes sneezed with excitement when their handlers came to them; they barked to each other, yelped in pain, growled, whined, or sighed. But the greatest depth of communication the men and dogs shared was in silence.

In those pairs that worked at it, there grew a burgeoning, mutual comprehension. Eye and body movements and gestures took on greater significance. Studies have shown that dogs can read humans better than animals that are otherwise considered more intelligent than dogs, including chimpanzees. In this shared silence, an energy developed between them, one that became more palpable every day, and especially with every mission. These were among the things that Carter observed, and privately measured.

Though Carter knew not all handlers achieved close unions with their dogs, it was not his job to condemn or praise these relationships. The dogs were equipment, he had been taught, and were to be kept in combat-ready condition. That was his job.

His gentle hands, soft, quick voice, and sharp intelligence offered him the tools he needed for his work. Not only was he skilled, his manner nurtured a strong trust from both the men and the dogs. Like many of the young men there who assumed the mantle of medic for human soldiers, Carter projected an ease, a confidence, and even a maturity that established strength and integrity in his position. He flowed naturally into his role as dog medic. He even sometimes helped out with humans in the LZ Sally field hospital when they were shorthanded. With the dogs, though he told himself he was simply maintaining equipment, he would never seem to be handling artillery. The men looked up to him, and the dogs endured him, even if they occasionally bit him.

Minutes after Jake's handler slunk out of the tent, Mercer, returning from his final mission with Dusty, pushed his way in. Carter was seated at his desk by now, eyeing the stacks of paperwork—food inspection forms, requisition forms, supply lists— and glanced up. Mercer stopped in front of him, his face a tangle of emotion: anger, betrayal, bewilderment. His clothes were caked with sweat and dust, and he smelled rank. Carter set his pen down on one of the piles of paper and waited.

Chris shook a small, red, wet plastic bag in his face.

"This what you want?"

"Sorry?" Carter drew back.

"This is what you asked for, isn't it?"

"Where's Dusty?" he asked, with immediate regret. Chris slapped the bag onto the desktop.

"Take it."

"Christ, Mercer. Take it easy. What happened?"

"It's the ear, the fucking ear. I cut it off, just like you assholes wanted me to. So here it is. You can mark it down on your little card there. Dusty is dead."

"I never said that. This is completely unnecessary. All you needed to do—"

"Bullshit!"

"Look," said Carter, his voice quiet, even. "If you say the dog died, then the dog died, alright? Chris?" He touched the bag. It was warm. He could barely see the ear for the blood that pressed against the clear plastic.

Mercer crossed his arms against his chest and dropped his eyes to the floor. He wanted to say more, to really yell at Carter. He'd planned a whole speech in the helicopter. It was going to be about all the bullshit, all the not caring about the individual, all about nobody having any say, about the dogs getting just more of the treatment they all got. Nobody cared; they were just bodies in service to the killing.

But suddenly everything drained out of him. He was too tired to think, or speak, or try to right any wrongs. He couldn't say anything at all. He felt the reality of his youth and his utter impotency in the face of the institutions that controlled his life. He felt the uselessness of saying anything to anyone. He saw the loneliness and smallness of Carter's job there, and he could only turn around and walk away, banging his dusty steel pot against his leg.

Jonathan Wahl wandered in with the mail and saw Carter staring up from his chair, wide-eyed and blinking, after Mercer, who brushed wordlessly past him.

"I don't know what I'm supposed to do with this thing. Is there even such a regulation?" Wahl spotted the bag and knew not to ask. Carter looked away, then over at the mail in Wahl's hands.

He missed Sue, her wavy blond hair, her open blue eyes, her soft manner of speaking and moving. And he was not disappointed. Jonathan left the tent, and Carter took a clean scalpel from among his instruments to open the letter. After he read it, he folded it neatly in three, returned it to its envelope, folded the envelope in half, and slipped it into his breast pocket, where it would remain for the rest of the day, until he read it again that night, and stored it away in the box under his bunk. He pressed his hand over the pocket to feel the contents, then returned his gaze to the bag.

Mercer had labeled it, evidently after the ear had been put inside since the writing was jumbled and crooked, "Dusty, poisoned by VC." But Carter suspected the dog had more likely died of heatstroke; he'd seen so much of it lately. Rusty had recently had Sig medevacked in from Mongoose when he showed the typical symptoms.

Warned by the radioman, Carter had been waiting for Sig and Rusty that day. They'd doused him with the water and lowered his temperature, then given him a few days to regain his health. Powrzanas had rushed Pal in once for the same thing, and they'd had success then too. Later, when Pal was poisoned, there had been little question of the symptoms being anything other than poisoning.

Intentional poisoning of dogs by VC was rare. More commonly, poisoning occurred when dogs got into American supplies—antifreeze, fuel, or explosives. Heatstroke, though, remained the greatest killer, and handlers had a responsibility to watch out for it. Even though it may not have been their fault, still they assumed guilt if it happened. If their dog had to die, handlers wanted it to be from something unavoidable--in the line of fire, or enemy poisoning—nobler deaths. Of the 4,000 documented dogs who served in the Vietnam war, only about 250 were killed in combat. Carter pulled Dusty's card from the box, marked heatstroke as the cause of death, put it back in the file, and placed the bagged ear in the trash.

Wahl returned, poking his head into the tent, "Come on, John, we need to take a jeep to Phu Bai." Carter nodded in assent. "We're going to collect Otis and Bagatta's dogs."

Wahl held the door open as Flexi jumped in, scrambled onto the back seat, circled, and lay down. Carter and Wahl got into the jeep, Wahl driving this time. They passed through the gates of the camp with its body-count sign proudly erect, and bumped down the road to Phu Bai with bursts of red dust shooting up behind them.

"Otis's legs are pretty messed up, but I don't think he lost anything. And from what I understand, Bagatta may be headed back to the World."

The two men had a routine trip ahead of them. They would pick up the dogs—both uninjured--and bring them back in the jeep. Carter would check them over, and they would be returned to their stake-out area, where they would be fed and given water. After that, they would be assigned to a handler who was without a dog for whatever reason, or Carter would tend to them until they were needed.

For Otis, a harrowing trip lay ahead, as hospital after hospital transferred him to more sophisticated facilities.

He would never blame Rolf for missing the mine. The greens were tangled and thick, riding up and grabbing their legs, and the men on the line were spread out across the horizon, impossibly hoping to detect every deterrent laid out for them. Otis hadn't stepped on a mine, just been too close when someone else did. When Otis felt himself floating backward, before the pain began to register, he spread his broad hands out, the leash gliding away from him, Rolf leaping high and away. Then flat on his back, Otis sensed the heat creeping up his legs, instinctively grabbing at them and rolling onto his side. He heard other pop-pops and screaming swirling into the chopped greens and dust and sulfur, a stew filling the air. Then a dark form over him, the medic hovering, the sweetness of the morphine, shadows of the chopper blades, and hot, tumultuous sleep, indiscernible from wakefulness, in and out, then wind blowing over him, and away.

He was first taken to Phu Bai, then Danang, and finally Yokahama, Japan, where doctors would work to save his legs. Rolf had been left in the kennels of the vet detachment in Phu Bai, to wait.

The day after Otis's injury, Frank Bagatta, working with Rebel, was wounded during one of the missions off of Mongoose, under identical circumstances: sweeping near the Eight-Klick Ville in a horizontal line, another soldier stepped on a booby trap. Burning shrapnel landed in Frank's leg. It was Frank and Rebel's second time out. Frank had been sent directly to Japan.

Rebel was uninjured and joined Rolf in Phu Bai as Frank made his way to Yokahama. Neither handler knew anything of their dog's condition or whereabouts, nor were they in any shape to think of them. It quickly became clear that Frank was not coming back to the unit. He would be sent home, while Otis lingered in Japan for treatment and recovery.

Within days, the dogs were pacing and eager to get some work. Both were teamed up with new, available handlers. Rolf would go to a handler whose dog was among those not able to work under combat conditions, and a few days later, Rebel would become partner to another dogless handler, Jimmy Powrzanas.

Jimmy dreaded teaming up with another dog after Pal, but as soon as he began working with the foxy Rebel, he could see that the others had been right about him. Rebel was a push-button dog—smart, quick, obedient, cool and composed, and sure in the execution of his duties. He was lively, but not boisterous. He was precise and dignified. Any handler would be thrilled to have him.

But Jim was different now. He watched the dog go through his paces in practice workouts, and he admired him—his beauty, his skills, his performance—and he was relieved that he'd gotten a good dog. But he felt himself pulling away, building a wall. He would feel reassured in the field, the dog would be a good scout, but he wouldn't let it get beyond that.

He could see that Rebel was sleeker and tighter than Pal, and he couldn't help making other comparisons as well, though he tried to push those thoughts away.

He and Pal had started from scratch together, both green, both hard workers. Together they'd trained and made the long journey away from everything they'd known. They had walked point together, and they'd made important finds. They'd been together on their virgin mission, when he'd held Pal down in the firefight, and held onto him for his life.

Pal had been his dog, heart and soul; they'd worked and lived as one, and without knowing it, he had let that dog get inside him as nothing else had. When Pal died, there had been no time for grieving, and no understood way to grieve for him. You just absorbed it, and moved on. Jim didn't want to allow that emotional attachment to happen again. He would remind himself that Rebel was only a dog, only a way to stay alive until he could go home and be normal. He would just get through it from now on.

The dog Jake continued to mend, though the process was hardly one of John Carter's more rewarding efforts. Because the broken leg would take weeks to heal, the handler had been assigned another dog, and Jake became John Carter's temporary responsibility. As they began to build an uneasy friendship, John would relax and gain confidence in the animal, believing he was getting through to him. Then the dog would turn on him with angry teeth. But John persisted quietly, maintaining the dog on his routine.

Choppers were dropping in and out of the landing strip on a sultry August afternoon as Carter snapped the leash onto Jake's choke collar for a walk. Jake was by now staked out with the other dogs, his cast removed. John walked at an easy pace, leaving the leash slack, sauntering, and together they observed the goings-on around the dusty base. He stopped to chat with Larry Proper, setting off for a nearby village for a social visit.

Proper had befriended some children there. When he'd left for Vietnam, Larry had not felt solid with his new wife. He worried that she might not be able to stand the quiet married life he'd envisioned for the two of them. But shortly after his arrival in Vietnam, she'd written to say she was pregnant, and his hope for their future was renewed. Jim Powrzanas had the same news from Nancy, and the two men grew closer. They felt a new maturity, an urgency to return home, and so Larry felt a kinship for these village children and wanted to protect them. He began to visit their house to help out with repairs, bringing small gifts too.

John chatted easily with Larry as Larry packed up some cokes and candy for the kids. He barely noticed Wahl walking by. But Jake, and not for the first time, seized the moment. He lunged, and Wahl, seeing the flash of teeth in time, jumped back. Carter was startled, let the leash slip, and Jake took off, with a series of loud, exhilarated barks that could have been shouts of glee. He

charged toward the dogs' area, which ignited with replies to Jake. Flexible, now grown into early adolescence, trotted out of the command tent where she'd been lying under Wahl's desk. When Jake spotted the off-leash animal, he stopped himself short, skidded in a half circle, and headed toward her in a determined beeline. Wahl dropped the sheaf of papers he'd been carrying in horror and dashed back to the scene, but Jake was ahead of him and closing in on Flexi.

The puppy stood watching, head cocked. As the dog neared, she dropped onto the ground, her white underbelly smeared with clay dust, tail thumping. When Jake got to her, she offered him her neck. Jake froze, tail curled up high, a ridge of hair bold upright on his back.

They touched noses. She rolled over. He made a tiny hop in place, then another, then began, stiffly, to wag his tail.

Flexi jumped up, and they spun together in a friendly, frenetic whirlpool of dirt and fur and saliva until Wahl and Carter arrived to grab the collars and restore order.

If Jake had made it to the other dogs, a full-blown fight would have resulted. Unneutered male dogs identifying with a territory, in this instance the perimeters of their individual doghouse and stake-out areas, would naturally have put all efforts into defending it from any trespasser. But even Jake, hardly a dog to give breaks, recognized the vulnerability of Flexi and made the choice not to attack her. Was it her youth, or, perhaps, her gender? All female scout dogs were spayed as they entered service, so Jake would not have come into contact with a reproductive female since he'd become a military dog. Flexi had not yet been spayed. Perhaps Jake stopped out of curiosity, his aggression circumvented by Flexi's being a female. He had certainly stopped himself from his first intention of fighting.

Jake would go on to more scouting work, but the perpetually gun-shy Tramp would not. For dogs such as Tramp, the trip to Bien Hoa meant a period of retraining or, if the dog was deemed truly unable to perform, a destination at the main vet detachment at Tan Son Nhut. There the dog would serve as a blood donor for other dogs, or be euthanized. As with any military dog that died, the vet there would perform an autopsy. He would send blood and tissue samples to Saigon for further examination, and the dog would be cremated. His medical file would contain comments from the vet, including any information concerning the cause of death.

Carter would not be apprised of the dog's eventual fate. He simply managed what was handed to him. Like regular human medics, he did whatever he could at his level, and then if more was needed, handed his patients up to the next. He was an integral part of his platoon, and his world did not extend beyond it.

Notes

$5,000 value: "Med. Care of VN War Dogs," *Journal of the Am Vet Med Assn.*, 1970, p. 405.

88 days, Jeff Cahen.

99 days, Cliff Searcy.

Wade, Nicholas, "From Wolf to Dog," *New York Times*, 11/22/02.

Captions

p. 137: John Carter.

p. 138: At the Veterinary Detachment in Phu Bai, Sergeant James Selix (left) and John Carter.

p. 143: Bert Hubble and Butch.

p. 146: Jonathan Wahl.

p. 151: Jeff 3M61, Tom Corsello's dog, with one of Flexible's puppies.

# Boonie Hat

First squad remained at Mongoose from mid-July until the end of August. Otis was recovering in Japan, Frank had returned to Brooklyn, the World, and Joe McMahon was named squad leader, though he did not try to emulate Otis. He was better known for throwing out beer cans over the river and letting his dog, Alex, soar out to catch them before they hit the water.

As the weeks passed, they hardened to their conditions, the heavy heat, occasional deluges of steaming rain, fearless rats, and swarming mosquitoes. Pearce continued working to be accepted by the guys — the other handlers and also the regular troops they were assisting. Whether he grew to prefer this outsider way of living, or whether simply afraid of the sergeant who teased him mercilessly back at Sally, Pearce hoped to delay his return there. Things were looser out here, fewer people knew him well, so fewer saw him as the butt of jokes. Here he was with infantry, practically one of them, or so he saw it.

Pearce liked things better at Mongoose, way out and away, living off the elements. He was as good as any of them here now. He and Prince had a rhythm on the trail, automatic and in sync. Pearce was proud. At last he was living the part he'd so longed to play. As their time at Mongoose drew to a close, he volunteered to replace the dog team scheduled for the last day's mission. The others readied for their return to Sally.

Packing his rucksack that morning, Rusty had watched as Pearce rolled up his sleeves into neat cuffs and smoothed his hands over his chest.

"Hey Asshole, don't wear tiger stripes out there."

Pearce patted the beloved, sweat-salted uniform and smiled. They had belonged to Rusty earlier. Rusty had

bartered for them, offering cold beer to a Long Range Reconnaissance Patrol unit passing through Sally in exchange for a set of their signature tiger-striped fatigues. Pearce had taken one look at them and gone wild, pestering and pleading until Rusty gave in. He let Pearce buy them from him for twenty dollars.

Beside the tiger stripes, Pearce also kept a special hat, which he had not dared bring to Mongoose. It was a wide-brimmed Australian outback hat. Australian troops served in Vietnam from 1965 until 1971, and Australia was also a coveted destination for R&R adventures. The hat was among his most cherished possessions.

Pearce had taken great care with this article. First he'd sewn onto it, by hand, the cloth patch with the insignia of the 101st Airborne Division, with its Screaming Eagle image, that also had the 47th Infantry Platoon Scout Dog banner stitched into it. Then he had soaked the hat in a mixture of water and starch, pulling it out and shaping it with one side up, the other flat out, and then drying it in the sun to the perfect jaunty form. It was carefully boxed and under his cot at Sally now. Today he sported his regular soft bucket hat, his boonie hat.

"And wear your steel pot. Jesus." Rusty was soon on

a chopper and thankfully returning to Sally. Pearce waved as the others of the 47th lifted out.

When he gathered up with his assigned unit for that day, the guys continued to raze the easy target. They had nothing particularly against the guy; it's just that they knew him to be the goat. They could also feel the adulation, and seeing themselves as the lowest men in Vietnam, they got kind of a kick out of it.

"Hey Pearce, if you're going to be a real grunt for a day, put on your pot."

"Don't be a pussy, Pearce."

The LT merely pointed to the boonie hat. Pearce stuffed it in his pocket.

He and Prince were on the trail minutes later, patrolling along the paths of the Eight-Klick Ville.

There was Pearce, determinedly clomping down the path. His boots, impossibly large for his awkward, willowy frame, slapped duck-footed on the dry trail. His gun hung loosely from his arm, and in an act of confidence, he had let Prince off leash. He knew the dog would not stop working, and he did not. A mine had been discovered and detonated earlier that day along the trail by another patrol. They entered above that section.

Pearce was accompanying a small patrol consisting of part of a squad from second platoon. C Company had set up a base camp between Mongoose and the Eight Klick Ville, along the trail, and had been using the dog-man teams on daily patrols. The idea was to keep small, squad-sized patrols relentlessly scouring the trails and bush. That way, NVA troops could never get fully dug in. They could harass them, but never truly become ensconced enough to control the area. It was a frustrating and bitter duel, with constant prowling, setting up of night ambushes to catch them working the trails, and constant discovery of booby traps, which were then steadily and quickly replaced by NVA. The pressure became both routine and excruciating, as boobytraps were too frequently found the hard way.

So keen was the anticipation of the traps that, a few days earlier, one of the squad members had tripped one, leapt into the air, and literally outrun its explosion. Knowing their enormous likelihood of coming across the deadly contraptions, their humor turned dark, and that episode, when recounted over evening C-rations, became no more than a joke to them, or at least it was told that way. The tension and the fear worked their way into them, becoming part of them. And they grew very fond of the dog teams.

When the dog teams came along, it was not like getting a new guy, an innocent cherry in a fresh uniform. The dog teams now knew the area, knew what they were doing, and were seasoned, regular guys. This company also knew how to use the teams. This lightened the load for all of them.

Today, there were seven men, counting Pearce, with Pop Watson sharing point with Pearce and Prince, and they had seen little. They were relatively loose, which meant they were alert, but shy of intense. Pearce tossed wisecracks with the guys.

Things had gone quietly on the trail that day, and they were returning in the afternoon, as the light grew sharper and the clouds seemed to lower onto them. Prince weaved in and out among them, joyfully sniffing, feet lifting crisply with each step. Pearce was no longer walking point, leaving that to Pop, a 37-year-old enlisted man. He was about mid-way in the line, when Prince froze into an alert ahead of him. They all froze with him for a second, and then someone said, "It's nothing. That's the one the other squad detonated this morning."

"What's the matter with your dog, Pearce? Only find day-old traps?"

"Can't he smell?" Much laughter, while Pearce also laughed as if he were not embarrassed. But Prince continued in his circling action, swinging behind Pearce, and seconds later, nose waving, haunches down onto the ground, Prince froze into another alert signal.

Pearce instinctively snapped his head around to have a look, and could see the trip wire. He called out the alert, but not in time to stop the infantryman who triggered it. As the explosion shouted into the air with all its hot debris, Pearce and the others did what they were supposed to do; they dove into the brush. But as they were diving, Pop, at point, tripped another trap strung across the path. The explosion shot up between his legs, and he was killed nearly instantly. Shrapnel had also hit those first, second, and third in the line. And Pearce was flat out and unconscious. The impact of the first explosion had hurled Prince over Pearce's head, but he appeared unhurt. The two at the end of the line, Cliff Searcy and Lou Savoy, were the only uninjured men.

Earlier in that same day, when the other squad had passed along this trail on their way out, they had discovered and then detonated that boobytrap, the scent Prince had first alerted to. But fresh ones had been planted. Neither tripwire had been there. They were less than one hundred yards from the company command post.

Cliff could see that Pop was dead, and though he'd known the older soldier longer, and felt the bonds of brotherhood with him, he knew, by now instinctively, to rush to the aid of those still possibly alive. He spotted Pearce, then hesitated, turning to Savoy.

"If that dog comes after me, shoot him."

Pearce did not have a drop of blood on him, but when Searcy went to give him mouth-to-mouth resuscitation, cradling Pearce's head in his hands, he felt a small slimy patch, and then saw the pale gray of a piece of Pearce's brain. *The hat,* he thought. *He must have switched back to his boonie hat.* It was one of those details you remember in a moment of trauma, a mental note, an accounting of your circumstances and surroundings that sticks with you forever.

And then he remembered the dog. Cliff was afraid of dogs even in the best of circumstances, and so, in the middle of this, he worried about the big dog.

He knew it was Pearce's habit to bait the dog, to goad him into aggressive acts toward outsiders. That pleased Pearce, and Prince had tasted more than his share of new troops strolling across Sally. But now was different. For one, Cliff and the others were not new to him anymore. Prince could understand they were familiar and respected people, even if they remained wary of him.

More perplexing, the dog had no idea what to do or even what was expected of him at this point. Never before had he been called on to choose his behavior, and under such conditions, with the noise, the smells and confusion. He looked to Pearce for guidance, leadership, a familiar command, but Pearce was blank. So the dog reacted according to his own mind.

Prince did not attack Searcy or try in any way to block Cliff's efforts to revive Pearce. When Cliff next looked up, he saw Prince, not frantic or barking or rushing toward him, but only walking deliberately to Pearce, then collapsing his legs under his body, like a folding table, and dropping down to position himself by Pearce's side, quiet and alert, with ears erect and slender long arms extended in front of him. He remained stationary, attentive, and in the perfect down position, guarding Pearce.

Cliff saw confusion and fear in the dog's eyes, but Prince remained calm and motionless, as if he were in shock. And then Pearce began breathing. They were so close to their camp that by then others, hearing the explosions, now arrived, and the medic, and others from their unit, quickly pitched in to help.

The medevac helicopters rushed down into their space; then the shouting, the lifting and confusion of loading the wounded, the blurred movement, as Pearce, accompanied by Prince, and the other wounded and killed—all of the patrol except Cliff and Lou Savoy--went away, straight up.

Carter was playing cards in the command tent with Wahl, both men not really listening to the radio, tipping back in their chairs to study their hands and toss cards onto the table.

"Wait up," said Wahl, settling his chair, laying his cards on the table, face down. He turned around and raised the radio volume.

"Yeah, we've got one killed and four WIA down here. One's a dog handler." A chill went through them as their eyes met. The cards were forgotten, their stomachs contracted, and they began the wait, hoping to see Pearce soon. He was the only one left at Mongoose, so they knew who the transmission was talking about.

Curt Knapp was leaning back in the pilot's seat of his Huey, on the ground and waiting at yet another battalion field camp. He was the pilot for Colonel Hoefling, commander of the 2nd Brigade. They moved over the brigade's entire Area of Operations, dropping in to check plans with company or platoon officers, flying over to survey a mission's progress, hovering here, landing there, making sure all the pieces were moving ahead as they were supposed to do, Hoefling adding his expertise, or just experienced opinion, where he felt one could be offered, sometimes dropping off supplies as well. Knapp was on the ground now, waiting as "White Owl" conducted a meeting.

Knapp had enlisted in the Army, eager to fly, and within a year he was in the air. He didn't love the war, but he loved flying, zipping through the air in the Huey. One of his favorite games was "Concentration," flipping over a card, then recalling its match from previous turns. Knapp could spot a clearing, then commit it to memory. He knew this area's intricate topography intimately. But there was little action in his current, privileged job as Hoefling's driver. He spent a lot of time waiting.

And that day, as he sat idly in the Huey, listening to the giant radio console behind him, he also heard the frantic transmission that Carter and Wahl had just heard, and he recognized the location, the patch of trail. He'd flown over it not half an hour earlier.

He sat up now, aching to be part of the rescue instead of just doing the usual cushy work. Out here it was embarrassing, almost unmanly, to have such an easy job as his. While the majority of those in the war might not have considered Knapp's job as being "in the rear," he knew the I Corps grunts, in the field day after day, saw him that way, while they took the weight of the war. And he knew he had more in him than that.

He hesitated. Hoefling was in that briefing, and he'd likely be in it for a while. If Knapp ran in and interrupted, what were the chances the Colonel would allow him to go out and help? What if the medevac had trouble finding the exact spot? What if the unit were being fired on? He had plenty of gun power in his bird.

He contacted the medevac and raced to the site. They swooped in one after the other. Knapp sucked in a deep breath, nodded to his crew, and dropped down. Searcy had grabbed the M-60 machine gun and was firing like a crazy man at the nothingness out there. Knapp looked up from the confusion, handing over one, then grabbing after the next wounded soldier, and suddenly found himself face to face with an enormous yellow German shepherd dog.

Knapp was aware of the fact that there were dog handlers in the area, and he'd even heard the transmission saying there was a handler among the wounded, but it had all happened so quickly that he hadn't thought much about the dog. Knapp and Hoefling were headquartered at LZ Sally, but at the opposite end from the dog unit. They knew of the scout dog program, but had little contact with any of the individuals.

The troops heaved the dog up after Pearce and ducked away from the roaring downwind of the Huey's blades. Knapp flinched. Nearly one hundred pounds of ferocious dog in the loud, cramped hull of the Huey, with the wounded men lying by his feet--as pilot it was his call, should he refuse to take the dog? He'd heard how possessive some of them could be, that they sometimes wouldn't allow people to touch wounded handlers. The dog and the man met eyes. No time to ponder—"Take that leash and tie it to something," he shouted over the din, and lifted up. The crew exchanged glances and headed for the hospital at Phu Bai.

And there was Prince, still beside Pearce.

After boarding the helicopter, he'd been tied up near Pearce. He jerked his head up and down, resisting, in a panic at first, then settled down. His eyes glazed over, and he eased himself carefully along the corrugated steel floor, nails scratching and tapping, again into a down  position, his front legs like two straight lines before him. He stared stoically ahead and never moved throughout the flight. Remaining as close to Pearce as possible, he seemed neither to hear anything nor to notice the other men around him. Still and silent, frozen into position, he was panting in great heaves, as if his chest would burst.

---

Notes

Figures for Australian participation: *Encyclopedia of Vietnam War*.

The Australians also participated in the Combat Tracker Team program, using Labrador retrievers to follow ground scent in pursuit of fleeing enemy. See Haran.

---

Captions

p. 156: Marvin Pearce, with puppy Flexible.

p. 164: Frank Steinhebel's dog, Bullet 6M29, looking over Phu Bai (in 1970).

# Finding Prince

In the small patch of shade provided by a flap of canvas at the front of the tented barracks, Larry Proper gripped the stubby brush and pulled it through Fellow's black coat. The morning air was thick and hot, the red dust kicked up in waves as the helicopters slipped in and out of the landing strip next to them, thin human shouts barely etching into the din. He'd exercised Fellow, fed, and watered him, and now their favorite time had arrived, the dog sitting, tongue stretched out in panting, eyes closing, mouth a gaping grin of pleasure. Again and again Larry pulled the brush through, great wads of downy undercoat, like shredded cotton, flying into the air and stuffing the brush bristles as if creating mattress batting, until Larry had to stop and pull it, a fist-sized black pillow, out of the brush and toss it aside, then go digging into the coat again.

How could a body have so much hair? Both now breathing together, relaxed, How could there be so much of it? He brushed and pulled, the dog off and on slapping his foot against the ground in ecstasy. Does it stop? Does it ever stop? This'll keep him cooler. Jimmy's out now. With Rebel, Frank's dog, and Frank's gone, back to New York City. I couldn't live there. Too bad about Pal. Too bad Jimmy had to watch him go like that, be there and see it. I'll be careful. I'm not letting Fellow drink but what I've got for him. And I'm keeping his coat as thin as I can do. I'll brush and brush till it's all gone and he can be cool. I take care of you and you take care of me. Just as we've been doing. We've been okay so far. I don't want a new dog. I could be switching tracks in Erie right now. I could be learning my trade, maybe getting promoted. I didn't ask to be here, didn't ask for a promotion here either. I got one anyways—Spec 4. I don't know what I'm doing here, but we're here alright. We've been doing okay though, doing okay. Wonder why I don't hear from Patty.

Another thumping of choppers. Larry looks up.

"Hey."

"Hey, Jimmy. How'd it go?"

"Fine."

"Okay." If Jimmy and Rebel had been in a firefight, or found 400 pounds of rice, or alerted on twelve boobytraps and a sniper, the answer would have been the same. Larry knew that. They were safe, and that was all that mattered then. Jimmy sat down with all his weight onto his cot, then fell back with a sigh, staring at the tent ceiling. They'd go for a coke in a little while.

In the command tent, Jonathan Wahl scrunches over his typewriter, thick, black-framed glasses sliding down his nose in the heat, sleeves rolled up as tight as they can go, belt buckle digs into the flat waist; thin already, the heat is making them all thinner still. He squints and grimaces to push the glasses up, but they slide down again. Isn't the dry season supposed to end soon? Sometimes his fingers slide on the shiny flat plastic of the black keys. He is typing the letter to Pearce's parents.

He met Pearce's mother once, back at Fort Benning. He is not sure Mrs. Cook, as Pearce's mother is named because she got divorced and remarried when Pearce was a kid, can even read. She seemed so fragile, thin and weathered as an old woman, though she was barely in her thirties, blinking at them then, sliding the chrome-plated 38 over to Pearce, Here, hon, you'll need this. This the one you asked for. Yes, ma'am, answered Pearce, beaming, hiding it among his possessions, his comic books and sling shot and other items he'd thought he'd use with his buddies, friends who had never really materialized.

Wahl had had to go through all those possessions again, those objects of Pearce's dreams — the knife, the Australian hat, the soldier magazines, the beer glass from the bar in Bien Hoa, was it his first beer? A pack of cigarettes, never attempted. He had to pick from among them and pack them neatly into a box to send home to Mrs. Cook. And home was in a small beach town in California, not Fort Worth, Texas, as he'd told them. He'd wanted to be from Texas, like Rusty. The body had gone home for the burial in Santa Cruz, and he and Lt. Stockdale were learning the duties that were part of what happened when you died over here. After this, a division chaplain was coming to have a service, and what else could they do?

They'd forgotten about the dog at first, in the shock of it. When they remembered Prince, they didn't know what had happened to him. That was another thing they would have to deal with, what to do with the dog, and where was he, or was he even alive? But for now, it was Pearce. They had to finish the work involved with being dead in the army in Vietnam, when you died on August 25, 1968, at eighteen years of age.

Lt. Stockdale wasn't sure how to write the letter. He wasn't a big talker, but in this case he was not the sort of person just to say the minimum. He wanted to make it personal. He hadn't met Mrs. Cook, but he was close with his own parents and tried to imagine what it would be like to get such a letter.

Was Pearce's death his fault? Hadn't he told Pearce over and over to wear his helmet? Why hadn't he? But you can't say that in the letter. He would say what a good dog handler Pearce had been, what a good soldier, how he'd always been ready to put out the effort. All that was true. But he was such a kid, the youngest of them all. He could be a jerk, but he was basically the baby, and they all felt that sense of responsibility to him, that begrudging sense that even if he could be a pain, they couldn't let him hurt himself. Stockdale always held the safety of his men far ahead of any self-promotion. He was only getting through his job here, not trying to prove anything. He wanted everyone to be okay, not to get hurt. And he'd let Pearce down that way.

The doctor who took care of Pearce had been surprised by his death. Pearce was alive when he'd arrived at the hospital ship just outside Danang, unconscious, but alive. He had a small injury to the brain, but this was going to be manageable, the doctor thought. He could patch this guy up.

Minutes after he came in, Pearce went into shock. The nurse was yelling in his face to revive him: What's your name, Private! Where're you from! Who's the President! Come on, wake up.... But he could not fight his way out, could not step out of it. He sank, and he gave in. There was nothing to call on for the superhuman leap back into life. He was only Marvin, after all, and no more. No John Wayne, no comic book hero. In the end, though he'd tried to be tough, his innocent softness provided him no reserves.

"He did not have the will to live," the doctor later told Stockdale. "Physically, he could have lived. His mind was not strong enough."

Stockdale had not disliked this job. He was fond of the dogs. The men liked the dogs. It would be okay, except people started getting hurt. Well, what did he expect? First, Otis. Otis! The last one he expected.

Otis had somehow been the arms that embraced all of them. He'd argued for them and with them, comforted them, listened, cajoled, laughed. He'd urged them on. There was a naivete, an enthusiasm, all his. There was exaggeration, tall tales, even out-and-out fantasy, but there was an undeniable, unspoken, and genuine love for each individual—dog or man—and they all knew it. They would never say so out loud, but they missed him.

Then Frank. That kid was coming along so well, developing such a good attitude, now gone home; but he'd be okay.

A week later, Harraden. What an awful mess. Stan could still see him on the litter coming off the helicopter—his head hanging over the side of the stretcher, his mouth running a streak. He was not conscious of the bloody mess below his waist--and all of them thinking, Why did they bring him here to this little field hospital? Then nervously waiting for the next chopper to take him to a better place, to try everything for him. Then Youtz and Jonson, also wounded, even if lightly. Each and every one of them victims of booby traps, either directly if the dog missed them or, mostly, from fast-moving and merciless rockets of flying shrapnel, someone else having tripped or stepped on the thing.

And they'd lost dogs too. Youtz's dog Willie, from the booby-trapped bomb that had also hit Youtz's arm; Tramp, who was finally sent away when any hope of the terrified animal's being useful finally fizzled out;

Mercer's dog Dusty, from the heat; and Pal. That one had been especially bad. Jim was different after that. Always very cool, he was a little cut off and more determinedly workmanlike after that. Hell, where was Pearce's Prince anyway? With Pearce gone, it suddenly became terribly important to find what remained, the dog. A small piece of the kid could come back to the unit.

Stockdale held the letter as typed by Wahl. He looked it over, looked away, and crumpled it into a ball. He tossed it into the wire basket.

"I've got some revisions," he told Wahl. And Wahl knew it would have to be perfect, and they would be there some time yet.

When the chaplain sauntered over to their camp area, Stockdale sent Wahl out to round up the guys.

"Do you need any information on him?" Wahl asked before heading out.

"Nope. I'm all set," the chaplain answered.

He stood firmly, blinking over a perky smile that poked into round red cheeks, in the small tent, benches in lines in front of him. He began quickly with the Lord's Prayer, moved on, not missing a beat, to the death service, a generic Protestant rite, and ended with a clipped, even hurried, rendition of the 23rd Psalm. Before they could summon up the appropriate sentiment or even reflect on what had happened here, it was over. The chaplain scurried out, back to the command area of Sally, maybe for a beer or a game of cards.

The men stood silently for a minute. No one knew what to say. That was it? Stockdale coughed. He put his hat back on and stalked out of the tent. The rest of the unit filtered out, all vaguely unsatisfied, unquenched.

Rusty: "The little punk deserved more than that."

Everyone knew what Rusty meant. They had lost a member of their family, and no one seemed to care.

In the silence that followed, the men suddenly felt a glimmer of understanding of what was happening within themselves. Pearce, least likely, least liked, had managed to touch them and surprise them. In their grief over the first fallen member of the group, the men discovered a unifying consciousness. Pearce awoke a realization and then an understanding of their kinship to one another, to their dogs, to their mission there that transcended any personal differences between them. The injustice of his impersonal memorial service only strengthened their sense of self-containment, of being together outside the main system. They discovered their own community in their grief, and they recognized the supreme intimacy of their unit. The silent connection they had nurtured, each between himself and his dog, had grown. It extended between and among the men too, and suddenly they saw it, as families sometimes recognize the strength, or the absence, of their ties in tragedy and loss. The men had been able to transcend the differences between species to form an intimate bond with their dogs; now they saw that they had done that with one another as well. Without consciously trying, in fact barely noticing it, their hearts had grown, had expanded, in ways that would remain with them for life. That growth had given them pain at times, but loving the dog had expanded their humanity.

Stockdale climbed into the chopper. He wanted to walk Pearce's last walk so he could write the letter properly, whether or not Mrs. Cook could read it. And he needed to find the dog too. They swooped in over the village east of Hue.

"It's near here."

He found the unit that had been out with Pearce that day, or what remained of it. They showed him where it happened, and he saw the grass, the bamboo, the languid river, the trail.

As he walked alongside Cliff, they talked about how Pearce would not have been injured wearing his steel pot. None of the men who were there that day forgot. "We wear them without fail now," Cliff said, "and no more crying about it, either."

"What about the dog?"

"The dog?" Cliff nodded, remembering his hot panic looking into the eyes of the confused animal. "The dog was fine. It went with him in the chopper."

Stockdale flew on to Phu Bai, Pearce's first stop. He went to the veterinary detachment.

"Yeah, I remember it. Somebody brought in a dog from a wounded handler a couple of days ago. If he's not here, he was reassigned somewhere."

"Could you check?"

"It could take some time."

Stockdale went for a beer. He sat at a tiny table, alone, in his limp fatigues and dusty boots.

There was little to recommend Phu Bai. Row after row of tented hooches, red dust, army green, jeeps rattling by, loosely organized basketball games, the occasional pair of nurses walking, heads together, dressed in fatigues. Phu Bai had suffered damage during Tet, and reconstruction of parts of it was still underway.

Stockdale was determined to bring Prince back.

Last time he'd been here, things had not gone well. He and Carter had brought Brown Dog here to be euthanized. Though the dog had performed well in training, he proved a failure in the field. Three handlers had been wounded walking with him, each on their first mission. Either the dog missed everything, or he was unreadable. No handler would get near him. It was the only recourse at the time. Stockdale had accepted that. What a waste — the wounded men and the loss of the dog as well.

The ride back to Sally in the truck had been somber. Without thinking, Stockdale had agreed to give a lift to an infantryman they didn't know. The guy was obnoxious, chattering like an idiot the entire time. They ignored him. Finally the guy lit up a joint. Stockdale had not paid much attention to the insignificant amount of grass smoking he'd seen around the base, but just at that moment, affable as he normally was, it grated on him. Right in his face, a sign of disrespect to an officer. When they got back to Sally, Stockdale had reported the incident to the man's commanding officer. But it hadn't made him feel any better. This time he would come back with the dog. He was determined.

When he checked back at the veterinary hospital, he was told the dog had been handed over to another scout dog unit, the 42nd, operating out of Camp Eagle, which was a few minutes drive northwest of Phu Bai. It had been easier than keeping him at the vet detachment, taking up space and supplies and time for his routine care. He wasn't sick or hurt.

"Could you get me a jeep? I'll be back in twenty minutes."

Then Stockdale put in a few more calls. There was another place in Phu Bai he needed to visit today. He'd just found out about Otis. Otis was okay, and he was on his way back to the unit. He was in Phu Bai at that very moment, resting on a hospital bed in the Phu Bai medical detachment.

Otis had almost been sent home. For five weeks lying in his bed in Japan recovering, Otis had thought he'd be headed home. That's what the doctors had said, and so that's what he thought, too. A bad knee had taken him out of professional football; now this, the smashing up of the knees, even worse than before, would send him out of Vietnam. He had toyed with the idea of staying in the army. He could still do that, even with this. He'd be behind a desk somewhere stateside, and that would be alright. He'd grown up near Ft. Benning; it would be natural.

But those who controlled these things—the government and the army--had other ideas; the war was taking another shape. They were pumping more and more men into it, so even though Bagatta had gotten to go home, the time Otis took to recover brought him to a more restrictive set of criteria for going home. Instead, he would come back to the unit, and be used to train the replacements that were beginning to flow in.

They were already talking about rotating the handlers of the 47th to different areas, where the need for experienced handlers was great. In a few weeks some would move out, with their original dogs, to a unit in the delta area down south. Even before they left, some new handlers would come in, guys who hadn't been trained together or with them, new guys who would pick up where they left off, who would take up the extra dogs and make them their own. They'd trained with other dogs at Ft. Benning and then come over empty-handed to take the dogs from handlers who were leaving, or were hurt or had died, or got moved to another job.

When Otis was hit, he didn't know what had happened to Rolf. But Rolf was fine. He'd been reassigned to another handler when that man's dog was injured. It would hurt when he saw them together. He knew that. He was no longer a handler.

Otis had also worried about those he'd left behind in his squad — Rusty, Pearce, and the others. He had had a strange and unexpected sensation of being cut off, just leaving them there.

Stockdale appeared, standing next to him, holding his hat in his hands. Otis looked into his eyes, his voice like a soft bell.

"Mongoose was a hell hole. Why did we get sent there? I will never understand that." Stockdale gave Otis a quiet nod. He hadn't liked sending them up there, had hated to do it, but theirs was the tightest squad, Otis the strongest squad leader.

"You heard about Pearce," he said, and Otis's face contracted.

"I sent him into that mission."

"You were already hurt then."

"It was like I did it."

"Otis, the new guys are going to need your expertise. It'll be okay. Come on with me. Let's find Pearce's dog."

Otis pulled himself out of the bed and stood hesitantly. Stockdale could see that it hurt him to move. He began to walk gingerly out. Neither said a word.

The 42nd and the 47th had a working relationship. They bunked up at one another's facilities when teams needed to stop off in each other's locations on the way to or from missions. From time to time they traded or borrowed supplies from one another when they ran out and resupply was not yet forthcoming. They knew one another maybe not by name, but often by face. They recognized in one another their mutual mission, their unusual experience there. So though there was at first some reluctance on the 42$^{nd}$'s part to give up the strong and willing dog, they understood where the dog belonged. And in the end they let him go to his unit.

When Otis and Lt. Stockdale got back into the jeep and headed up to Sally, Prince was with them, stretched across the back seat in all his golden glory. The dog knew Otis, and let the men handle him easily. As they pulled up at the unit, dust puffs rising up from the tires, from under the hood, Prince looked around—did he expect Pearce? Did he understand? Do dogs make assumptions about their lives? They thrive on order and routine; they like knowing precisely what is expected of them. But their ability to adapt and go forward is astounding, a remarkable part of their nature.

That is not to say their loyalty is fickle. It is eternal. Stories of dogs who return to the site of their master's last appearance for years, or even the remainder of their lives, do exist. That loyalty never dissipates. But eventually most are able to accept the alternatives that are offered to them. Like a new artery that grows after an old one is severed, they rebuild new passages of affection and obedience, from which grows a new loyalty.

But how did the dogs experience their handlers' departures? Did they await their return? Those who have lived in a close relationship with their dog know the answer: Of course they do. It is a permanent attachment. They wait, just as they wait at a closed door, staring, still, until someone comes along to open it.

Otis's stomach churned—the mixture of returning to

the unit with apprehension of what was to unfold for himself there now.

But those thoughts were sideswiped by a noise he heard cutting through the air. Rolf was barking to greet him. He could not see or hear him, yet somehow Rolf had felt his presence, recognized his return, and Otis knew, out of all the noise and barking, Rolf's voice. Stockdale couldn't know that Otis was hearing it, but Otis knew. It went straight into him, as did the knowledge that Rolf was no longer his dog. He knew he would have to stay clear of the animal. That hurt.

"He's going to Mercer."

"Rolf?"

"No, I mean Prince. I thought it over, and I think Mercer should be the one to take Prince."

"I see it that way just fine. It's good." Otis took the leash. "Who's got Rolf?"

"He's okay. He's with someone else now, Ernie Jonson. It has to be that way. You know Ernie will be good with him."

"I'll put Prince up," Otis offered, leading him over toward the kennels.

"Otis, you're going to have to get used to it, you know."

But Otis was already thinking, Rolf was my heart, my eyes. And when he led Prince to his stake-out area, just an excuse to get a look at Rolf, Rolf went a little nuts, recognizing Otis, throwing himself the length of his line, leaping and barking, eyes shining and expecting with his entire body a reunion that would not happen. Otis did what he knew he had to do. He turned and walked away. The ache was awful.

He would explain to Ernie how Rolf was good at

spotting mines on trails, how he was good in the high heat, but that he was less adept at finding caches of weapons. These things and more: Rolf's unusual alerts, how he liked to be handled. All these he would explain. It would be okay. He could adapt; the dog could adapt also. With their huge capacity for love, it was possible, and it was necessary. But would the deepest bond be with the one who had trained him, who had shaped him into the dog he was today? Would he remember that? Would he feel the loss as Otis felt it? Or do dogs simply move on, adding to their history of connections, enrichment, enlargement of the spirit?

Otis knew, as they were all now understanding, that this was not a time for sentimentality. They all had jobs to do. The dogs were soldiers just as the men were. They worked together, each in his best capacity. And the dogs wanted to do their jobs as soldiers.

And so Rolf would move on, continue in the work of a scout dog, to get it right again and execute with his innate and encouraged abilities his exhilarating, dangerous job. And Prince also would find new happiness after Pearce.

---

Notes

Pearce eventually kept the 38 in the arms room, as he was supposed to do. He would check it out periodically, and, instead of using it for practice shooting at the range, would instead head out into the woods and shoot it at will.

Communalizing grief, and the need for grieving: Shay, pp. 39, 65.

# Defiance

*It spoke not only of boys and dogs, it spoke of other things we were feeling as well. It spoke of the intense loyalty we felt toward each other, and it spoke of our own growing sense of mysticism. Our trust of instincts was growing into a worship and we had formed a family tribe where anything was possible.*

Nathaniel Tripp, FatherSoldierSon

Extraordinary changes, silent and invisible, had altered the handlers: their interactions with the dogs were expanding their capacity for communication, friendship, forgiveness, and forbearance. They were barely aware of it, but the changes would last a lifetime. Their entire war experience would transform them from boys or young men on the cusp of maturity into the full-fledged beings they would remain for life. It set them. And whatever hardness might have been forged into them by combat would be ameliorated by their camaraderie with one another, and by the lessons taught by the dogs. Their humanity was enriched when they reached into another species, and found something there. That delightful surprise sparked hope and a broader consciousness.

Now, though, what they understood was that it was their dogs' hearts' desire to prove themselves again and again in the field, that they would give all they had in them to get it right. And the handlers knew exactly how much they did have in them. By now each handler knew the intricate points of his dog's skills and vulnerabilities, as each man also grew more aware of his own. Together, they had accomplished much in their time there.

As the end of 1968 approached, the platoon had

completed 778 missions. Beginning with the first patrols out of Mongoose in July, the men and dogs had faced the varieties of challenges to be found among grassy coastal plains, the searing beaches, the boot-sucking rice paddies, the villages of dubious loyalty, the dense mountain jungles, and the elusive topography of the A Shau valley, favorite hiding place of the NVA. They had also spent several weeks supporting a unit stationed near the DMZ. The dog-men teams had so impressed those soldiers that they had asked to be given their own scout dog unit for permanent support. While the scout dog teams were credited with the deaths of thirty-two enemy and sixty-four prisoners so far, the many lives they may

 have routinely saved were not among the statistics, even though their real strength and purpose was the protection of U.S. lives.

Among the finds: Rebel, working with Jim Powrzanas, had uncovered a large U.S. bomb hidden in the ground outside a village; it was wired by the NVA to be tripped by approaching U.S. troops. The soldiers cleared the area and detonated the bomb harmlessly. Another time, and deep into the night, Rebel alerted with a soft growl from the top of a bunker overlooking a bridge on the Song Bo River. Illumination rounds were set off, and VC with "satchel" charges were spotted and driven away with machine gun fire and grenades. Satchel charges were suitcases of explosives intended to be tossed into sleeping or staging areas. No one in the group was hurt.

And the scout dogs and handlers weren't the only

ones blossoming and maturing. Flexi, the small, black-and-white mascot, had come of age too. The men began to notice her swelling sides. Spaying hadn't occurred to them, and she'd encountered several of the scout dogs in her rounds of the camp. Soon her pregnancy grew large, and Carter and Wahl thought she seemed uncomfortable and sluggish. They were a little perplexed about delivering puppies, or if they needed to do anything at all. The father would have been so much larger than Flexi, maybe there would be problems. A trip to the vet detachment seemed logical. A fresh load of beer and maybe some other delights from Phu Bai would be nice too. Flexi was comfortably settled on the back seat of the jeep, and Carter and Wahl drove off.

The vet in Phu Bai inspected her and determined that delivery was several weeks off. "She's healthy, though. Not to worry. Need some steaks?"

On the return trip, Flexi became more restless. The road was potholed and bumpy. The dog was jostled as they lurched along. By the time they'd gotten back to Sally, Flexi had moved to the front seat, climbing over Wahl's lap and then down into the floor space between his feet. She was circling and crying.

"Something's happening down there," said Wahl. He lifted his feet. "There's blood." Soon the head of a puppy began to emerge.

Carter sped into the camp, and the two men carefully lifted the dog up, carrying her, and the first, still wet, puppy, into the Carter's vet tent for the remainder of the delivery. Eight pups were born. All survived, and all appeared mostly German shepherd. They were given away to soldiers passing through Sally, who tucked them into their shirts and carried them off to become mascots around the area. The 47th kept one puppy and called her Sally-J. Their pet dog had given birth, spread her presence, and they felt the pride of their own legacy.

But even though the dogs and handlers felt themselves now seasoned and efficient in their work, there was still sometimes trouble convincing the regular infantry units they supported of their effectiveness. The dog teams could not promise one hundred percent accuracy, though it was usually through improper use of them that people got hurt. What had changed by now was that the handlers had gained enough confidence in their own and their dogs' skills, and in what lay around them, to understand that they knew as much, and sometimes more, than some platoon leaders.

Because of the rapid rotation of officers, platoon leaders were often new to their jobs and had little, if any, knowledge of the terrain, much less of scout dogs and their usefulness. The regular soldiers who were out day after day also knew more than many of the lieutenants who gave them their orders. This began to build a new bond between the line soldiers and the handlers, some of whom they began to recognize and know personally.

A lieutenant, possibly not knowing exactly or entirely what he was doing anyway, might have been ordered by a commander to bring this alien element, this dog and this man he'd never seen before, along with them on a mission. And he was supposed to give over his men, men he was only beginning to know, to a dog? Relinquish the faint security he felt in his newly acquainted point man to a dog? It only added to the insecurities of their job. It was one more place he had to guess, and pretend he knew what he was doing.

But the dog handlers knew when they were right.

Now they were ready to speak out about it.

At the end of September, Lt. Stockdale invited Colonel Hoefling and others of the Second Brigade command to a formal demonstration of the talents and uses of the dogs and handlers at their area in Sally. The men polished up the practice obstacle course to better illustrate the variety of finds and maneuvers and skills of the dogs and men working in the field. Stockdale selected Rusty and Sig as the pair to showcase the quickness and athleticism of this work. When the day arrived, the team smoothly showed off their best stuff, never missing a dummy or obstacle, and those at the top order were duly impressed. Rusty beamed and swaggered as he led his big dog off the field. If only his father, who had never advanced far in his own lifetime career in the military, could witness this. Colonel Hoefling requested a manual from the unit, which Jonathan Wahl produced, detailing the dog teams' capabilities, when they were best called for, and how to utilize them most effectively. The manual also included the history of scout dogs in the military, and their care, and had an illustrated cover. They believed this would straighten things out now, and people would understand them better.

But only those at the top had attended the event, and only they saw the manual. Those who most needed it did not have access to it. The platoon leaders who would be actually running the missions and using the dog teams were not available for base camp demonstration events. They were out working in the field. So the wrong people got the best information. When the top brass sent out missions, and thought, Yes, an excellent time to add a dog team, only they understood the relevance of it. It was rarely translated to the platoon leader or company commander, who, following orders, continued to carry along these extra beings, often baffled about the point of it all.

Such was the raw lieutenant Rusty faced in December, through the thick downpour introducing the rainy season.

His face was hard and set, but at the same time the fresh lieutenant seemed almost to flinch from the responsibility that had landed on his shoulders. He was merely hours old to the job. To best cover his jumpiness, he jutted his jaw upward, hand on his hip, and strutted among the men. All of them had been there longer than he had and knew the area well. They were perfectly aware of the tenuousness of this leadership, were girding themselves for a rookie mistake he would soon be likely to make. Who among them would pay the price for it? This was the third change of leadership for some of them, those whose tours were winding down. They just wanted to get out, and they didn't want a hyper-anxious maverick to keep them from getting home. And so they were pleased to see the familiar dog team arrive.

At Sally, Rusty barely noticed the undulations of the grass from the arriving helicopter wind. As had happened so often over these months, minutes earlier, Sig had stood, knowing the craft was coming before Rusty had caught any outward signs, and had started the leaping that so aggravated Rusty. He lept up, as high as Rusty's head, knowing the ride was about to begin, that he'd go up where it was cold. As the helicopter touched down, Sig dragged Rusty along, jerking him up behind him, with Rusty yelling, "Kiss my ass, dog," at him, and then, on board, immediately heaved his heap of bones with a klunk onto the metal floor, and spread out, relaxed into it, and sighed, oblivious to the noise or the rocking and soaring movements that carried him.

Even though it was winter and the rainy season, it was still hot most of the time. Only now, instead of hot and dusty, it was hot and wet. The dogs didn't like the wet. When they weren't working, but standing out in the rain, it was customary for them to try to climb inside their handlers' already steamy ponchos. The handlers would then be wet, hot, and covered with wet dog hair, most particularly wet dog hair smell. Still they did let them into the ponchos.

Rusty had also been there long enough now to recognize the new-car smell of the lieutenant. He was too clean, his uniform's rich green color still unfaded. Rusty been with this unit before, and was welcomed back as one of them. They liked the dog. They wanted to pet the dog, see the tricks, watch it do something silly.

But when he got there, they went right to work, not surprisingly finding nothing in the rain. Night began to fall. They stopped on the trail, about fifty yards from an abandoned village.

"Alright, set out the claymores." The men paused and looked at each other through the veil of rain, then unfolded their shovels, and began digging in for this soggy night position. Rusty, however, resisted. He felt apart from the others, practically equal to the LT. He wanted to stand up for himself and for the other guys.

"That just makes no sense. We should set up in the ville. That way we can sleep in the hooches there, get dry."

"This is the place." He had followed the map, thought he was doing right, but now knowing he had probably done something stupid, and shown his greenness, the lieutenant started to stalk away. Then he turned to Rusty, "Dogman, you take first shift."

"I ain't pulling guard duty. My dog will get tired. He has to work tomorrow." Rusty knew Sig would guard the group through the night, and he didn't mind pulling

guard duty himself, but he had a point to make here.

"You're up." The LT stopped and turned, dreading this challenge, hoping not to lose the men's respect on the first night.

"You check that little book of yours," Rusty answered. "Dog handlers and their dogs ain't supposed to pull guard duty."

"I can court martial you, Allen."

"Bullshit. You don't like it, you can call me a chopper right now."

He made ready for sleep. He tied Sig's leash to his leg as he always did for sleeping in the field. He lay there in the rain and observed the others through the gray-black wetness. One man, already asleep, floated away on his air mattress off of the trail.

He saw the LT stir and stand up and begin to pace around them. He felt Sig tighten up. He turned onto his side, laid his head flat, and pretended he was asleep. He closed his eyes and smiled.

The LT was walking in his direction, not to him, just to the side of the group of men where they were dug in. Sig felt the tension surrounding the LT. He suddenly lifted his big head, a look of surprise from officer and dog in this meeting of two pairs of shining black eyes, and with a light *yip,* Sig went for him, lunged after him. Rusty still pretended to be asleep. His sleeping bag made a sled, Sig pulling him through the slime like a mad reindeer, Rusty laughing now, unable to hold it back, the LT's fears of his men and of the NVA, of responsibility and RPGs dissipated with the snarling black-and-blond giant charging after him. He screamed once, like a girl. That was all Rusty needed. He hauled Sig back to him, and curled up with the dog. No one said a word.

The next morning they set quietly about their usual work, walking ahead. They were moving out to set up an ambush in a wooded area, but needed to cross a large rice field to get there. Late in 1968, the Americans were aware that the NVA were preparing a second Tet offensive for early 1969. They knew they were infiltrating this area, gathering up for a new attack on Hue. These small patrols were being sent out to search for them, and then to ambush them, before they themselves were detected and ambushed.

When they had waded half way through the muck of the rice paddy, Sig alerted to the tree line on the other side ahead, and by the strength of the alert Rusty knew the place must be loaded with NVA. Sig grew skittish, jumpy, growling softly and casting his gaze all around. They were about 750 yards from the tree line, and now they could see there was also a deep canal there in front of the woods.

Rusty turned to those behind him, "The place is full of gooks."

"Keep moving," came back to him from the LT.

At two hundred yards from the canal Sig began to rear up, pulling at the leash. Rusty looked back. But the

LT had been told to set up an ambush in the woods, and that was what they were going to do. He told Rusty to go on. Rusty refused.

The LT sent up two guys to check it out. They stopped at the canal and came back.

"We can't cross that canal. It's too deep."

"Go on acrost it."

"We'll be wet up to our necks. Shouldn't we go around it?"

"We got to go through right here." The LT was crushing his map in his hand, hoping he was doing right. By now the entire squad had moved up close together, all staring in a tight half-circle at the nervous LT, and leaning in toward him.

"Look, Lieutenant," said one, "the dog team is saying there's personnel up there."

"I am giving you an order," the LT could barely rasp out the words to Rusty.

"Kiss my ass, I ain't going," declared Rusty, "and you can court martial me if you want to."

"I'll have all your asses."

But one of the men answered, quietly, "We'll kill your ass right here."

And the LT, after some deliberation and struggling to breathe naturally, said to his radio operator, "Call in and tell them this is not a good place to set up an ambush." He paused again, then said, "We'll move down a few hundred meters and set up down there," and slogged away through the paddy.

The next morning they approached the intended set-up area from the side. There they saw the flattened and matted mounds of elephant grass, where the NVA's machine guns had been set up. They had been pointed directly at them yesterday, and those NVA soldiers had been poised, just waiting for them.

_____

Notes

*47th IPSD Commander's Briefing.*

Stories of Jim Powrzanas and Rebel: *Army Times,* reprinted in *Dogman,* vol. 4, no. 6, p.1.

_____

Captions

p. 182: Rusty Allen (left) and Jim Powrzanas.

p. 188: Sig.

# Replacements

*Our storm-battle for life brought him to light, and through him as through a window I have ever since been looking with deeper sympathy into all my fellow mortals.*

John Muir, Stickeen

Dropped into a tiny, blown-out patch of jungle, Larry and Fellow walked together up a short, knotty, misty slope to join the exhausted company, as twilight fell. They were in the mountains now. They were relieving the dogs and handlers already spent by this mission, now lifting up above them in the Huey, breathing their choked sighs of relief.

One of the unit's guys ambled over, nodded to Larry, and put his hands tentatively on Fellow. Fellow stood and wagged his body, enjoying the calm affection. Fellow had always been soft on people, even if he was not friendly toward other dogs. Encouraged, the man knelt and wrapped his arms around the dog. Fellow sat. Then the soldier buried his head in the dog's neck and held him tightly and for several long moments. Three close friends had been killed today and things would not be letting up any time soon.

In March of 1969 operations for the 47th began to move west, into the Ashau mountains. Military commanders for I Corps had shifted their focus to the area, knowing it to be riddled with NVA coming in from the north along the Ho Chi Minh Trail. Actually, they were pouring in, determined soldiers laden with supplies—rice, ammunition, tanks, the works. NVA units were firmly dug in among the mountains there and especially in the Ashau valley, the snug and protected area that crept toward the lowlands, hidden just behind a jagged fence of hills. And so the dog teams were sent to help find where they were hiding.

The men, dog handlers and infantry alike, had no big picture, had no idea if the current move was because of success in the missions along the coast, with its crazy-quilt of booby-trap infested trails, or just because. Operation Nevada Eagle, begun the previous May, had ended in February of 1969. The operation's statistics: US 175 KIA; 1,161 WIA; enemy 3,299 KIA and 853 POWs.

Their concerns focused not on why, only how many more. They were well into the second half of their time there, close enough to be almost "short," those magical last few months when leaders would try to keep them out of the field as much as possible, giving them rear jobs like resupply or training the new guys or dogs, or doing anything on the base instead of sending them out, trying to increase their chances of staying alive until they could go home.

A few replacement handlers had begun trickling in as early as November. By early spring, replacements were beginning to outnumber the original handlers. Lieutenant Stockdale had also been moved, in December, to become a training officer at the dog detachment in Long Binh. He was succeeded at the 47th by Roberto Miller, a more military-minded officer. Lieutenants generally served about six months in one place before being moved around, sometimes less. Men of all ranks were allocated and then reallocated in seemingly random fashion. Miller was bucking for the rank of captain, and pushed for missions for the unit, to improve his own standing with superiors. While some men found comfort in his more structured management, others resented the chances he took with them.

The dogs also rotated to new units, if not with their handlers, then just transported by truck to new units as needed. They would get new handlers and simply continue at it, working as they had done before. Otis's Rolf, Rusty's Sig, and Powrzanas's Rebel would all change units and handlers in the near future.

The new guys were not coming in with their own dogs. They had trained with dogs at Fort Benning, then had been sent individually, not as a trained unit, to any variety of places in Vietnam. The dogs also would be sent over haphazardly now, or would remain as training dogs, depending on the need and the quality of the dog.

And now, when dog teams were called out on missions, seasoned handlers would travel out with new replacements for intense, on-the-job training. The original handlers might come with their own dog, but in some cases the dog had already been assigned a new handler, and they would simply walk slack solo with them to offer their knowledge, and their protection.

Larry glanced around to get a sense of things. Here was an entire company, made up of three platoons, rather than the smaller platoon units he was used to joining up with. Smaller patrols would have no purpose here. There were just too many NVA out there to deal with. And so several dog teams would go out at once to walk with them.

This night, people were quiet; the air was gray, taut, sad. There was little eye contact among them. Rusty had been there earlier in the day, fighting the tangle of green across the trail as he walked with a replacement and his new dog on their virgin mission, and he was with them as they lost their innocence in the ambush that kept the unit pinned down for four endless hours.

Rusty's Sig was already with a new handler, and when a week ago Bernard Hrouda went out with Sig on his first mission, Rusty could not go with them. It would distract the dog. Hrouda instead was joined by Larry Proper with Fellow, Mercer now with Pearce's Prince, and another replacement, Don Jestes. When a unit called for more than one dog team, that meant the mission would be grueling, long, and so the teams took turns and were divvied up by the various squads and platoons. The dogs had to be fresh while they were working.

Jestes had received his dog King on his arrival at the 47th in the fall of 1968. King had just graduated from Benning, so they were both new. But it was not much of a match. The happy-go-lucky King had walked Jestes into ambushes on each of his first three missions. By the turn of the year, Jestes was having no more of it. He appealed to Powrzanas, whom he looked up to as an older brother.

"They can send me to jail if they want," he grumbled. "I'm not going out again with that dog."

King was sent to Bien Hoa to become a blood donor

for other dogs, and Jestes was assigned a new dog. Having been there a few months, Jestes had observed other handlers' dogs doing their jobs. He knew Jimmy Powrzanas was about to get out of the field, and he knew Rebel was the best dog going. Powrzanas understood what was about to happen. He was watching out for Don, and if it was time to relinguish his dog to stay on base now, he knew Jestes would be worthy of Rebel.

Jimmy had handed the dog over to Jestes, and walked away. The break was easier this time, not like with Pal.

Rusty and Powzanas, Otis also, were taking on administrative jobs, pulling away from the field. But it was not easy for Rusty to leave all of it to the new guys. Bored with the routine of base camp, he often volunteered to walk slack with the new handlers, covering the dog team as an extra pair of eyes and an extra gun. Something perverse urged him to continue going out. He had to know what was happening He might save someone, and he felt an uneasy need to be there.

Everybody called where they were now the Valley of Death, and it was. They walked into it day after day.

Some dogs were being trained to do their jobs off leash, to sit and wait for the handler to catch up with them as they alerted on the trail. Bizz, Leroy Jackson's dog, was like that, and when Jackson, on an earlier mission near this very spot, and having spent three days there already with contact on each day, stopped to rest for a minute on a small incline thick with trees, and heard the slide of a round being entered into a gun's chamber, he knew full well who was loading their rifle, that it was not one of their own guys. He dropped the leash and Bizz tore straight up the rest of the hill to identify the enemy, who opened fire. Bizz was killed instantly that day, but he saved the unit. The men had not been ambushed.

The lieutenant was spooked from the previous day's attack. He knew the dog teams were useful, but there was the continuing conflict that unit leaders had to contend with: putting the dog team, or his trusted point man, first in the line. The skills of the dog could save lives, could make missions more efficient, but they might also disrupt the harmony of the delicately balanced teamwork that existed between the men already there. Each fire team, each squad, each platoon, had learned to get inside one another, and also knew their individual jobs so well that when the firing began, movements so well practiced had become automatic. Orders were not screamed out over the din of battle; instead it was a silent dance. Everyone knew their place, knew what to do, could act without deliberating about it in the midst of frantic, chaotic, and unexpected conditions. The "plan" was never really a solid plan, just a place to take off from, just a starting point where everybody jumped from and into their conditioned choreography of panic. When the full power of the fear and the adrenaline kicked in, there was no thinking, only acting, instantaneous; and it was the way they knew best to save lives. The dog teams understood, even if it frustrated them. They understood because they were that way with their dogs. They acted as one, just as the seasoned infantrymen did with one another, seamless, deliberate movements in a swirl of anarchy.

So the next morning, when they began the patrol, and Larry and Fellow were with them, the regular point man walked first over the thin trail as they traversed the hill. He was followed by their slack man, and then came Larry and Fellow. Larry didn't argue. It wasn't in his nature to argue, and he understood what they'd just been through, how raw they were feeling. But he was nervous. Fellow trod on, working as usual, head going this way and that, scanning, moving, but with the point men swamping the scents that otherwise would have drifted into his sensory range.

The jungle was already a difficult place for dogs to pick up scents. The wet air, the dense vegetation, the curving trail with its dips and rises, all these worked in concert to diminish the dogs' access to the invisible scents hiding and drifting between the leaves. The cone of odor was broken in a million places. Still, the dogs did work on those trails, did find what was out there. Sometimes, though, and especially when the enemy was out there, poised, ready, knowing they were coming, the alerts came just too late.

And so it did that day also, as it had the day before. The dog was a hair too late, and the NVA got the bead on them. And everything happened again as it had yesterday. Bits of trees and vines flew and danced around them, chinging off their branches and trunks and floating to the ground. Then came the fury of dust and gunfire as sound and light became irrelevant, thinking became irrelevant, and they went into the drift of survival and attack.

But on this occasion, and for whatever reason, Fellow

lost his place in this disordered order. Who knows what clicked in his dog brain to say, Enough. His capacity to endure these conditions simply fell away from him. Larry needed to pick up his gun and return fire. No matter where he had been in line, he was an extra gun and he knew it, knew what he needed to do and what was expected of him. And he expected Fellow to fall in and stay close to him and silent. But the dog didn't do that.

Instead, infuriated and terrified, Fellow lunged toward the fire, seeming to launch his own personal attack at each round being fired, jerking Larry forward and adding to the confusion, throwing Larry momentarily off. The lieutenant, oblivious to the dog team now, sent the M-60 machine guns to the flanks to cover them, but with their tracers in full view, the shots enabled the NVA to pinpoint their quarry and shoot directly into them. Both machine gunners were killed. Wounded began falling around him as Larry struggled with the dog, whose full aggression and fear went into overdrive.

Fellow had been an aggressive dog from the onset; all of the scout dogs had to have that in them to get this far. And just as men say all their senses are most alive during combat, so the dog's senses intensified now, except he lost control, went over the top, and he had no ability to restrain himself, or remember his commands. Something in him snapped, and he lost the ability to hold onto rational behavior, learned, ingrained, deeply understood behavior, under these conditions. The same had happened to men under these same conditions.

But, as when men go berserk in war--committing acts they would never even remotely conceive of doing in civilized life, would consider abhorrent, completely out of the realm of their own identity as a human being--it was more than simply the dog losing control out of the fear contained in that moment. It was the accumulation of fear working on the mind, wearing down all that might hold him together. Time after time, month after month, the dogs had absorbed one horror after another, and they did not have the ability to comprehend when or if it would ever end. Even the men did not have that knowledge. It all just kept coming. The darkness, present in each of us, had been fed by the fear, encouraged by all the sights, pain, loss, hurt. The darkness had overcome his ability to think and reason and obey. A dog has little sense of "future" in any circumstance, and the continuum of war overwhelmed Fellow, and he snapped.

How had it come, and could it have been somehow prevented or assuaged? Fellow had gotten edgy lately, but so had all of them. Larry barely noticed it in his dog. Their friendship was unaffected, it seemed, or maybe it was deepened, by the life they were leading, as they traveled further away from civilized existence as they understood it. Throughout this journey, Fellow, like Larry, had continued to perform.

Only a few weeks earlier, while they were still working the coastal area, Fellow had put himself on night guard while Larry slept, during a nighttime ambush set-up in  small village. They were inside a school house next to a graveyard. Several VC crept across the yard, and the guard missed seeing them, but Fellow knew. He alerted, and the guy on guard, having watched the dog over the past few days, recognized the alert. He fired at the intruders and they dispersed. One was wounded, and his moaning weighted the air throughout night. They found him dead in the morning.

Now Larry put all of himself into his hands to hold the leash and keep the animal under control. The lieutenant ordered them back up the hill they had come around. Larry worried the dog would get hit. He worried he was in the way, making it worse for the others. He flattened himself onto the ground and began crawling backward, scooting, both hands dragging the hysterical dog, back and away from the fire. Soon he was unable to move and, after several efforts, realized he was backing into a small tree. He hadn't even felt it. He rolled away and slowly continued working back. As he did, he wrapped the leash around one hand and began grabbing fallen men, even with the twisting, writhing muscular dog, as if all of them were weightless, trying to get to an area where a medevac could land, could help them. He didn't know he was doing it. He didn't know what he was doing. It was his automatic reaction to the bodies lying around him, an automatic search for order in the confusion. And in the confusion there was no saying anything to the dog or trying in any way to settle him. It was simply a matter of trying to get through it alive, and helping the others who couldn't move.

Later, none of them were exactly sure how they had accomplished it. They only knew that after awhile, they were going back up the hill, that aircraft swung in and dropped 55-gallon drums of napalm, and that, when it was over, there wasn't an NVA body left to be counted. Six weeks later, the battle for Hamburger Hill would be fought on a neighboring hill.

The dogs did get excited in firefights and have to be restrained, but this time Fellow had endangered himself,

Larry, and possibly others. Larry didn't understand what had sent the dog to that new level of aggression, fury, but it worried him.

Several months later, Proper received the Bronze Star with Valor for his actions that day. He had seen more than enough for a lifetime, and soon he would be heading home, back to the World. But there was no such luck for Fellow.

The handlers were aware that no provisions had been made for the return of their dogs. Some had appealed to their congressmen or had tried to work deals with higher ups, but without success. Excuses given included that the dogs were unsuited for civilian life (though dogs were returned to families after World War II) or that they were carrying transmittable diseases that would endanger American dogs and possibly people. But the reality was that the dogs were classified by the military as "equipment," and therefore there was never a plan to return them to civilian life. Indeed, the plan was to keep them working there forever.

When handlers left, the dogs were reassigned; and when Americans left the war, the dogs were abandoned—reassigned to the reluctant and inexperienced handling of the ARVN troops, who were terrified of the dogs, and hungry for protein. For the lucky ones, there was euthanasia. Like so much else at the end of our involvement in Vietnam, most records of the dogs were jettisoned, or lost. There is no definitive accounting of the dogs—how many were there, what happened to them, who they were, though a former Army veterinarian, Dr. Howard Hayes, has been painstakingly recreating these records over the past thirty years. The fate of the dogs who worked during the war in Vietnam reflects the character of our exit from the war itself—sloppy, cruel, dishonorable: a betrayal of those who trusted in our protection.

Fellow didn't live long enough to face that end, though. That March mission in the Ashau was one of Larry and Fellow's last together. Larry was sent south to teach dog training to another unit, and Fellow was given to a new handler. Proper, like most of the handlers, never knew what eventually happened to his dog until some thirty years later. The gradual coming together of Vietnam veteran dog handlers occurred in the mid- to late 1990s, when the Vietnam Dog Handlers Association first took form. The internet became a vehicle for remote connections, and provided a private place for the rediscovery of others like themselves. Many created email addresses that reflect their Vietnam experience— their dog's name, their identity as a dog handler, or their unit affiliation. The warm surprise of recognition among brother dog handlers quickly gave way in each man to a desire to know the fate of his canine partner. Dr. Hayes was called on often.

Larry discovered that Fellow lived only about a month after they parted ways. He heard that the dog died as a result of a small arms fire, though the medical card that eventually surfaced has his death listed as heat stroke. Either way, the dog had little left in him. He had a rich life with Larry. Their year was full. Fellow was four at the time of his death, but with his experiences at war, he was an old dog by then.

Rebel died in July of 1969. He spent some months working in perfect synchronicity with Powrzanas. Don Jestes, who inherited Rebel from Jimmy, had been trained at Fort Benning in off-leash techniques, which

Rebel picked up right away. Rebel could work ahead of his handler, then run back to give him the alert. Jestes could snap his fingers and Rebel would return to his side. After working as Don Jestes's dog, Rebel was sent to the 58th IPSD, where there was a shortage of dogs, and assigned to Charles Decker.

In that unit another handler, Raymond Hales, was struggling with his assigned dog. Too nervous to go to the field with his own dog, and knowing Rebel's skills  and experience, Hales borrowed Rebel from Decker for his first mission. As they advanced along the trail, Rebel alerted several times, and the others saw the alerts, and hesitated. They knew the dog, had worked with Jestes and Rebel on several occasions. But Hales was not attuned to this dog. He did not recognize the signs. He was a green handler, unsure of the dog's messages, and without the confidence to stop the line of seasoned men behind him. Urged forward by Hales, Rebel obediently walked into the small ambush that was waiting for them. Man and dog were killed. Throughout Rebel's career as a scout dog, it seemed that everybody wanted him for his intelligence and high level of skill, but that no handler was personally attached to him. The young handler that day tried to follow the dog, but Rebel died with someone he never even knew.

Otis's dog Rolf went through several handlers, eventually making his way to the nearby 42nd IPSD, where Pearce's Prince had landed after Pearce's death, and been retrieved by Lt. Stockdale and returned to the 47th. Bill Bodnar was working with Rolf when they walked into an ambush in the jungle, July 17, 1970. The slack man was killed, and Rolf wounded. Rolf was medevacked to Phu Bai, but the shattered femur was "inoperable," and the dog was euthanized. Bodnar himself was unharmed. He brought Rolf's body back with him to the 42nd's base camp, Camp Eagle, and buried him there.

Considering that the handlers ranged in age from late teens to early twenties, and despite fond recollections of later decades, at the time the men were becoming short, their concerns naturally lay less with the fate of their dogs than with themselves. They simply accepted, with regret, that their dogs were not their own after all, and must be left behind. They were going home. That mattered more than anything or anyone else.

But coming home turned out to be less than expected. By the spring of 1969, antiwar sentiment was so high that the men were told to change out of their uniforms and into civilian clothes as soon as they landed in the States. Reports of American atrocities in the war were so generalized and wide spread that most returning soldiers were treated as pariah, and many found that potential employers were not interested in hiring them. The stereotype of the berserker Vietnam vet proliferated in books and movies. Eventually it was necessary for Vietnam veterans to be included in employment antidiscrimination legislation.

And it was not only the public hostility. Some veterans found life back in the States to be empty. The camaraderie was missing; and so were the highs of surviving combat. The negative reception they experienced on their return home, and the closeness, purity, and the rush of the life they had grown used to, drew some back. After a frustrating attempt at normal life, Rusty reenlisted.

Among other jobs on his return to the war, Rusty was a dog trainer with another unit, still within I Corps. In April of 1971, he came across Sig, by then with the 48th IPSD. Sig had gone through half a dozen handlers, and, reportedly, he had become "mean." When he saw Rusty, however, that was not evident. Despite his changes in handlers and the re-forming of connections, Sig still recognized Rusty, a fact that pleased Rusty then, but haunted him ever after. However many connections dogs form in the multiple families they often must experience, which ones matter to them? Do they all, or does the first mean the most? Which bonds are strongest? How long do they last? What do they mean to the dog, or to the human who has willingly broken them? The veteran handlers were experiencing the sense that they were betraying their dogs just as they also felt betrayed by this war. Sig was put down about a month after Rusty saw him. The reason is not recorded on Sig's medical card, but Rusty heard that the dog, at seven old for a scout dog, had been having trouble enduring the heat.

Despite the stated policy of the military, a few dogs did return from Vietnam to the States. Evidently, some of those letters to congressmen had hit the mark, or somehow the word about the abandonment of the dogs had gotten out. Bowing to political pressure, the Army made arrangements to ship a small selection of dogs. Stringent eligibility standards, elaborate quarantine periods, dipping and fumigating, and winnowing down of candidates produced four shipments of dogs back to the U.S. between April of 1970 and April of 1971. A total of 191 dogs made the trip.

Among them was a dog from the 47th, Pearce's Prince 14M1. He boarded one of those flights to the U.S., and continued his career as a military dog. The dogs were never intended to return as pets for families. The military felt that their training had made them too aggressive and difficult to fit into  civilian life again. So Prince remained in service until 1976, when, at ten years of age, he was euthanized with severe cataracts.

One dog whose fate is at this time unknown is the mascot Flexi (or the puppy the unit kept, Sally-J). When the 47th folded operations in July of 1971, both mascots were given to 2nd Brigade headquarters, where they retained their status as base pets. When the command left in December, according to a helicopter pilot with the division, no dogs were left behind. Everything, dogs included, was distributed to remaining units farther south. That is the last available information on the mascots as of this writing.

By the end of their tours, the men had lost their trust in just about everything, but those with close relationships with their dogs understood that their dog had never lost trust in them. They knew the dog would wait for their return, would have recognized them and welcomed them with everything they had in them, if they had returned. Finding out what ultimately happened to their dog came for most of them thirty years after the fact. It helps finish the picture for the handler, assures them that this is over now. The dog is gone. The war is over.

But what they also know is that the innocence that they brought with them into the war, the innocence they lost, never really left the dogs. The dogs learned from their handlers and led richer lives because of them. They in turn transformed their handlers' understanding of themselves, and of larger things as well. They drew from one another, and out of their connection, both became more than they had been or could have become.

There was a price to be paid for what the dogs gave their handlers. It is memory. The dogs waited for their handlers' return, and the handlers know it. In a sense, the dogs are waiting still, a small rock carried in the hearts of the handlers who let them in.

---

Notes

Miller pushing for more missions: January 121 missions; March 300 missions, After Action reports.

Dogs returning after WWII: Lemish, pp. 142-47.

Clark references to IHS and TCP: pp. 139-45; present in US for years, p. 150.

Clark references to disposition of dogs: pp. 14-53; refer also to Tony Montoya article; of the dogs who remained in Vietnam by the end of our involvement there, 371 were euthanized as "non-effectives" and 971 were handed over to the ARVNs.

---

Captions

p. 194: Jonathan Wahl and Flexible.

p. 195: Otis Johnson (left) and Larry Proper.

p. 196: Larry Proper

p. 197: Don Jestes with Rebel.

p. 205: Don Jestes and Rebel.

p. 208: Jonathan Wahl and Flexible.

# Coda: The Chosen Dog

Considering how intimately linked man and dog have always been, and that we know thoroughly the abilities of dogs for hunting, guarding, tracking, and even transporting, it was inevitable that the use of dogs in warfare would grow organically with our relationship. Dogs have been used enduringly as sentry, messenger, locator, and pack animals during warfare, but also for some practices that drew not on their naturally superior skills, but rather on their naturally inferior status within human society. Historically, they've been unleashed ahead of front lines to draw fire, directed into pitched battles to maul horses' legs, and strapped into spike-studded body armor to wreak havoc among enemy troop formations. As barbaric as those practices sound, modern usage hasn't always been fairer or more humane. Only more recently has the morality of these practices figured as a deterrent, and then not necessarily because the intrinsic ethics of such uses are questioned, but from fear of public outcry.

During the Second World War, Russians attached packs with twenty-six pounds of explosives over the backs of dogs, who were sent to enemy tanks (having been trained to expect food there) where the explosives would then detonate. The practice is said to continue to the present. The United States considered the use of such "suicide" dogs to destroy enemy bunkers during World War II, to the point of training some for the duty. They kept the project secret, referred to the dogs as "demolition wolves," and ultimately dropped it altogether. In fact, dogs serving in the Second World War appear to have been well treated generally.

With each major conflict, the U.S. military has garnered experience utilizing dogs in war, learning from European employment of dogs as well as their own mistakes and successes, though the mistakes were often forgotten in the enthusiasm over the successes. And completely overlooked has been the question of the ethics of using dogs in wars at all.

A dog is a funny creature: he occupies a unique, almost indefinable niche in human culture. He is not a human being, not even, as some people feel, a child. A dog can be similar, intellectually and emotionally, to a two- to five-year-old human child, but then some dogs will go on to develop a sensitivity from individually realized trails of thought and feeling far beyond a child's capacity, and others will never get past a primitive emotional or intellectual state. A dog is not a wild animal either. By his very definition, he coexists with man. Those who live in the wild are a separate species, and they're referred to as "wild dogs" when in that state, not "dogs," as elephants are called elephants, tigers called tigers, and so on, when they are animals in their natural state. Helen Marshall Thomas, in her book *The Hidden*

*Life of Dogs*, describes encouraging her dogs to slip back into a wilder form of behavior, believing that this would bring forth the dogs' "true" nature. But a dog's true nature is to be at one with man, to fold into our lives. It is through us that the dog is able to achieve the truth of his individual nature.

A comprehending and benevolent person will bring forth the greatest intelligence and aimiability in a dog, the interaction shaping the dog's persona. The mirror action can also be achieved--a loving friendship with a dog brings forward our own best qualities of patience, tolerance, humor, kindness, empathy, even a certain spirituality, or a spiritual curiosity, that results from attempting to connect to another species, a recognition that there is some kind of mystery in that synapse that exists between us.

Certainly a dog is more than a domesticated animal--a goat, cow, or sheep-- though many animals, these included, can become pets and thus become elevated through our interactions to a level beyond farm animals whose purpose is only utilitarian. Horses, because we've worked so closely together for so long, and cats, because of their intelligence and adaptability, come close to the dog in his unique category, but dogs, of all animals, are most naturally extensions of ourselves.

Our power over them is absolute. We've formed them into different breeds and assigned them tasks. They have little will over us except to disobey--and if we get tired of that, we dispose of them--or to run away and lead what according to all the research is a miserable

existence. For a dog, it's an incomplete existence unless they're lucky enough to get picked up and adopted by another human (not very likely--animal shelters rarely have much better than a twenty-five percent adoption rate). We no longer depend on them for survival as we may have done in cave-dwelling days. Even then, we could get along without them; they only made getting along a lot easier and perhaps gave us a leg-up in the evolutionary ascent. What keeps us together even now, when we seemingly need them hardly at all, is that mysterious synapse, the thing that happens in the connection. We're given an energy there, a spark that makes the relationship different from human relationships. A separate kind of trust can exist between human and dog: when the relationship is right, it's the chance, for some the only chance, to exercise complete, unwavering trust--not because it's as good as or better than a human relationship, but because it's *other than* a human relationship.

Is it fair, then, to send dogs to war? In the Vietnam war, a comparison between drafting men and donating dogs is particularly apt. For most of the men who fought in combat in Vietnam, there wasn't much of a choice. They were legally obliged to go. Young men who don't make political decisions are the ones best suited physically to fight the wars, and sending dogs is simply an extension of that moral reasoning. The young men are put forward to ensure our way of life. If they return, they will reap the benefits. If they don't, it was, presumably, worth the risk at least for their survivors and surviving generations. If that reasoning is acceptable in our society, then it is likewise acceptable for dogs and other dependent animals to go to war when they could perform duties that would increase the chances of a successful outcome to the war and also increase the chances of survival for humans doing the fighting. In Vietnam, dogs weren't used as an expendable  tool, but as a protective one, and they were treated carefully because they were valued as such and also were expensive to train.

From the beginning they did help us survive in wars. In World War I they, and dogs of all countries utilizing the Red Cross, located and assisted wounded men on the battlefield. They were critically important in messenger and sentry duties. They also carried weapons and even, in the case of Jack Russell terriers, helped rid the trenches of their notorious rat infestation.

The utilization of dogs by the military in World War II became more extensive and systematized. At the beginning of the war, we had forty war dogs, sled-dog veterans of Byrd's 1939 Antarctic Expedition. Most of these dogs worked in Greenland locating downed pilots, saving about a hundred men until the mid-1950s, when helicopters assumed the duty.

Having tasted the effectiveness of dogs in World War I, and, as significantly, having witnessed the dogs in service both to the Allied Europeans and to the Nazis, the U.S. military hoped to expand the employment of dogs in World War II. Creating a program specifically geared to working military dogs didn't come naturally. Indeed, at the time dogs weren't as commonly used in the U.S. for work in other spheres of American life, such as farming for example, as they were in Europe. Even obedience training for a dog was out of the ordinary. Consequently, there weren't many professional dog trainers to turn to in order to visualize, organize, and implement a military working dog program. But there was certainly a dog "fancy" in America, people who breed and show dogs, and some fanciers were particularly interested in the war effort.

Before World War II even more than today, the keeping of purebred dogs was a pastime that required money, travel, and the time to pursue seriously. A trip to Europe for the purpose of obtaining a well-bred dog, for example, was routine, as it still is for some breeders. People who kept kennels of pedigreed dogs were often the same ones who had stables of thoroughbred horses and who brought their dogs with them on shooting parties. In another example of the differences between the Vietnam war and World War II, patriotism for the latter knew no class lines, unlike the split that occurred, at least for part of the Vietnam war, between the blue collar worker and the intellectual of the 1960s. And it was blue blood rather than blue collar that would have characterized Alene Erlanger, a well-known breeder of poodles in the 1940s. In an effort worthy of a David O. Selznick movie, Erlanger pulled on her white gloves and pinned on her veiled hat to come to her country's service.

Immediately after Pearl Harbor Erlanger and several other prominent dog fanciers formed an organization they called Dogs for the Defense, and they barrelled into action. DFD worked on one hand to promote the notion of working dogs to the military, and on the other to recruit the dogs themselves from patriotic owners. It was one of those highly publicized, super-patriotic efforts that galvanized the ordinary man, woman, and child into action, offering them an opportunity to take part in the cause for freedom. Donating their beloved family pet to the military was  another sacrifice to be made with determined pride, like collecting scraps of metal, abandoning silk stockings and sugar, or planting a victory garden.

Dogs for the Defense's original idea was to recruit dogs for sentry duties, though other possibilities were quickly envisioned, and by the war's end dogs would be put to several, more specialized purposes. As the idea of a K-9 Corps, as it was unofficially known, took hold, procurement and training of the dogs fell into the hands of the Army Quartermaster Corps, though other branches of the military would develop their own procurement and training facilities, off and on. By the Vietnam era, procurement became centrally organized by the Air Force, since sentry dogs at air bases would be the most common use of the animals, while training, after shifting venues several times, ultimately became the bailiwick of the Army, at Fort Benning, Georgia.

During World War II dogs employed as scouts developed into an important facet of the military working dog program. Early attempts to use scout dogs in the European theater of war had fallen flat. The open terrain, the thunderous noise of battle, and the weather conditions of snow, mud, and heavy rain inhibited dogs' senses. Another, quite important drawback of battlefield noise was one that affected the men as well--the dogs were unprepared for and terrified, some shattered, by battlefield conditions. Trainers during the Vietnam era worked to condition the dogs to the sounds of war, but even so, as combat veterans can attest, simulated battle conditions bear only the remotest resemblance to actual firefight, and this continued to be a difficult point for the dogs to manage. They simply didn't understand it, though they did, for the most part, endure it, with varying degrees of fortitude.

Battle conditions notwithstanding, scout dogs were found to be dramatically effective not in the fields of Europe, but in the jungles of the South Pacific. Realizing their own dearth of training expertise, the Quartermaster Corps turned to Captain John B. Garle, of the British War

Dog Training School, and instigated under his guidance many of the training methods and uses of the dogs that would become further refined in Vietnam. Scouts weren't really put into use until 1944, so their potential only began to be realized by the end of the war. The demand for them grew quickly, so that messenger dogs-- still necessary, though less vital as radio equipment improved--were retrained into scouts and sometimes served in both capacities.

In the Dutch East Indies, in the Morotai Island campaign for example, the Japanese were driven into the jungle and, in small parties, made quick hits on U.S. troops. The U.S. was able to manage the tactics by dispatching reconnaissance and combat patrols led by scout dogs and handlers. Over six weeks, 250 patrols went out without once being detected. Knowing the effectiveness of the dogs, the Japanese would target them, something that would recur in Vietnam, where it was reported that the North Vietnamese offered bounties for killing U.S. dogs.

World War II commanders of regular infantry platoons who employed the dogs with their handlers would have a lot to learn about respecting the skills of the dog-men teams in order to best utilize them. They would need to learn the importance of briefing the handler at the onset of the mission, they would need to learn the capacities and limitations of the dogs, and they would need to learn to believe the dog, as interpreted by his handler. Ironically, though the dogs were accurate and effective, commanding officers of patrols in World War II would complain that the dogs slowed down the missions. This complaint would surface later in Vietnam, often with disastrous results when dogs' alerts were ignored.

One of the most generally accepted and implemented lessons about dogs to come out of World War II was the advantage of positive, reward training over negative, punishment training. Dogs proved easier to train and more effective in the execution of their duties when trained with praise and reward. It became in the military's best interest to be good to their dogs.

The same is true of healthcare and nutrition.  Better crates were designed for ventilation and protection from the elements, travel crates that could double as houses when the dogs reached their destinations. Fresh, better-balanced food was also beginning to be developed, though nutrient and water needs for the dogs continued to be studied and understood, a benefit of their military service that outlived the war. The dogs were plagued with many of the illnesses and parasites that would haunt the lives of the dogs in Vietnam-- heatstroke, skin diseases, stomach distress, hookworms, heartworms, and disease-bearing ticks among them.

There was (and is) still much to be learned about the sensory perception of dogs. In attempting to train dogs to detect mines, for example, trainers learned that the dogs were actually alerting to freshly turned (by humans) soil; had trainers realized the full capacities of dogs' sense of smell, they could have trained the dogs to scent the chemicals of the explosive itself. They did tap into other of the dogs' skills. For example, the Marines conducted a test where a man and a dog raced through heavy jungle. The man's time was more than fifteen minutes, while the dog managed the same terrain in less than five. Such studies would lead the way to encouraging off-leash training for scout dogs in Vietnam, although it wouldn't become standard until 1969. And they would need to refine the readings of the dogs' alerts. Dogs naturally alerted to animals as well as people, and the dangers posed by these encounters were another battle condition that had not been foreseen: the first dog killed in action in the South Pacific was the victim not of a Japanese soldier, but of a tiger.

Another discovery that experience proved was that when the dog spent most of his time with one handler, then the work was most effectively executed. Dog and man could grow to greater strength in their ability to communicate the more closely their bond was allowed to develop: not only was the dog-man bond natural, it should be fostered and encouraged. This realization led to a change in training techniques to allow for this communication line to develop. Man and dog would be kept together from earliest training and throughout their deployment.

Training was conducted together, and then the men were also permitted to spend down time with their dog. Thus the bond wasn't simply made of the ability to deliver and execute commands or of sending and interpreting alerts. Times of play and relaxation together strengthened the communion that provided an instantaneous thought-line between them. Besides, most of the men wanted it that way. The dogs were a great comfort to them psychologically and emotionally off the trail as well as during missions. When senses were heightened on a wartime mission, men and dogs would benefit by the bond they'd built over time and training. As happened often de facto during World War II and even more frequently in Vietnam, it is now standard practice for police dogs to live as well as work with their handlers. At least one soldier in WWII, Jesse Cowan, brought his own family's pet dog to the war as a working military dog, patrolling with him in Burma. Such a pairing would provide the optimum chance for sympathetic communication.

By late 1944, seven breeds had been singled out as preferred war dog types, crosses among them being acceptable: German shepherd, Doberman pinscher, Belgian sheepdog, collie, Siberian husky, malamute, and Eskimo dog. From this list, Doberman pinschers and German shepherds were most commonly seen, and the Marines preferred Dobermans. But a Marine report after the war concluded that, though Dobermans were highly intelligent and excellent workers, they were too "nervous" for battle conditions. German shepherds fared better in the report, earning praise for having "stood up excellently under field conditions; and throughout, their health average has been very high." This clinical assessment of the dog is capped by the statement that "possibly the fact that this group were not so highly bred may have had some bearing on their more stable qualities and better stamina."

With the sole exception of Labrador retrievers, who were used for tracking (bloodhounds having proven too noisy), German shepherds would become the working dog of choice during the Vietnam involvement. Those employed as scout dogs in World War II had demonstrated beyond any doubt their worth.

The breed had long been known for its wide-reaching working abilities. The American Kennel Club's official handbook, *The Complete Dog Book*, portrays the German shepherd as "First, last, and all the time a working dog...distinguished for loyalty, courage, and the ability to assimilate and retain training for a number of special services....Poised, unexcitable, and with well-controlled nerves....he must not be gun-shy and must have courage to protect his flocks...must and does exhibit a high order of intelligence and discrimination involving the qualities of observation, patience, faithful watchfulness, and even, to a certain degree, the exercise of judgment...power combined with agility...smooth and flowing...a natural dog." This description, when applied to a properly bred, trained, and utilized German shepherd, represents the ideal of the breed, but it is close enough to reality to convey the underlying potential of the dog. In fact, some disparage the breed for its workmanlike quality, believing there is nothing left of play or personality in the dog. Those who have lived and worked with the breed disagree, and have found that the dog adheres to the remainder of the AKC's description: "...he has plenty of dignity and some suspicion of strangers, but his friendship, once given, is given for life."

The comedian Jack Parr was in awe of his own German shepherd. Early in the 1960s, he had this bit (among others) about the breed: "They're so intelligent. They don't do tricks. Not like poodles. Poodles will do any trick you teach them. No, German shepherds. They're reading books, baking cakes." This appearance of independent intelligence may underlie the uneasiness some people feel about the breed.

The German shepherd's attitude differs strikingly from the classic image of dog as adulating servant of man. He does not engage indiscriminately, but he does adore. When the *handler* has earned the *dog*'s respect, there arises in the dog a quality that separates him from most other breeds. He possesses a nobility that is without arrogance, an electricity that is contained, a solidness sheathed in fragility, and when he plays, an intimacy that feels like a gift. German shepherds are sometimes unintelligent, but rarely silly. The dog can seem like a child prodigy that has suddenly been asked to stop talking or playing the violin or however else they express their innate brilliance: they often have that surprised, chastened expression. They are calm, but ever alert. And like every dog once he's been given the time and encouragement to express it, each has an individual personality, formed by their genes, by their experience and upbringing, and by their current handler or owner.

Threaded through their great nobility there is also, about most German shepherds I've seen, an appearance of some terrible sadness--not a droopy-eyed dog-sadness, but a poignant and secret weight, gracefully carried, as of one who has suffered some kind of unspeakable, irretrievable loss that we will never fathom. It may be a meaningless physical characteristic, but it's part of the mystery and the appeal of the breed. If memory can become absorbed into genes, then German shepherds, who've been war and police dogs as long as they've existed, could carry some material made of those memories, recurring genomic nightmares, that are a result of witnessing the darkest side of man's behavior. Could they be ashamed, and if so is it *of* us or *for* us?

## Coda: The Chosen Dog

The German shepherd has been around barely a hundred years, the creation of a German dog fancier, Max von Stephanitz. Von Stephanitz was a captain in the Prussian cavalry when his young wife, an actress, became embroiled in a scandal that led von Stephanitz to resign his post. He immediately turned his energies from horses and the military to his other passion, the breeding and raising of dogs. He became determined to develop the ultimate working dog from among the numerous farm and shepherd dog types. The array of types existed because farmers and shepherds desired dogs that performed their duties well: aesthetics or even uniformity of appearance were of utterly no concern.

He latched onto his new project with a passion, though he wasn't the first to conceive of the idea. Another group had started a club to develop the breed, but had disintegrated with infighting. There would be no such lack of resolution in the club formed under the leadership of Herr Rittmeister. He combed the dog shows for the perfect specimen--the most utilitarian size, the strongest yet most adaptable nature, the quickest mind and hardiest constitution. No consideration whatsoever was to be given to the aesthetics of the animal. On this point he was adamant. At last he singled out the dog Hektor von Linksrhein, whom he anointed as the father-to-be of the breed. He purchased the dog and renamed him Horand von Grafrath.

As the working dog template, Horand embodied the greatest, to von Stephanitz, of dogs that had been evolving over the centuries in Germany. Locals referred to the herdsman's dog type as the *rude* as early as the thirteenth century, when the work that dogs were being asked to do became increasingly specialized into such categories as boar hunting, herding, protecting livestock, and guarding property. Sometimes the larger-boned protective dogs were bred to the faster, lighter herding dogs in hopes of producing a more protective herding dog. Occasionally wolves were brought into the mix for intelligence and hardiness, a practice that continued for centuries. Dogs from the mountainous south tended to have heavier frames and longer coats, while those from the northern, central, and western areas were closer to the gray wolf--a so-called sharper dog, with finer features, a lighter frame, shorter coat, and longer stride. By the end of the seventeenth century, with wild game pushed outward and pastureland shrinking, the larger type diminished, though his lineage remained apparent. The southern (Wurtemberg or Bavarian) dog brought stronger hindquarters to the breed, while the Thuringian blood manifested itself through a vivacious character. Many of these latter dogs had wiry bodies and curled tails, characteristics that still spring up today in shepherds of wayward breeding.

Von Stephanitz founded his club--the *Verein fur Deutsche Schaferhunde S.V.*--along with fellow dog fancier Artur Meyer, on April 22, 1899, and Horand was duly named the first dog of the breed. Horand was described as the epitome of von Stephanitz's ideal dog, filled with joy and energy, fearless, alert, active, tolerant of adults, fond of children. Physically, he leaned to the Thuringian line. Measuring twenty-four inches at the shoulders, Horand was viewed a large, though not massive, dog. Today, that is the smallest allowable height for a pedigreed male. Horand displays other significant differences from what we expect to see in a purebred German shepherd dog today. The head is more refined, though the giant wolf-ears are apparent, and more striking, the back runs in a straight, long line, with no downward-sloping hips, and with the tail flowing in a natural line along the upper hind legs. The legs themselves are longer, straighter, and finer-boned than the dogs of today, and there is an overall compactness to the body. The dog does not resemble the Belgian Malinois, for whom some of these characteristics would apply. That dog is larger, and has a deeper chest, longer coat, longer legs, and smaller ears. The pre-World-War-1 German shepherd dog resembles today's dog mixed with a small, gray wolf, a look conveyed in all of the most important dogs of the early period--Roland, the first all-black German shepherd, Beowulf, Hektor, and Flora, a female often mentioned for the gracefulness and beauty she brought to the breed. Photographs of German shepherd dogs in the 1930s, and even beginning in the 1920s, reveal that the downward-sloping hips, tucked-under tail, and heavier-boned frame that characterize today's German shepherd were already beginning to be established. Among the early dogs, coat color had no bearing on conformation, and black, beige, and sable dogs as well as those with black-and-tan saddle markings competed freely.

Von Stephanitz refused to consider cosmetic attributes in his new breed. Though later, once the body type and characteristics had become defined, he "tolerated, however grudgingly, some effort to develop show beauty in the dogs, but he insisted until the end that efficiency should take precedence over mere beauty."

Von Stephanitz ruled his club with extreme discipline. In order to fulfill his vision for the breed, he decreed which dogs could be used for breeding and the number of puppies permitted in a litter. Culling was ruthless. He established the minimum age for females to bear litters and the maximum age for males to father them. With an experienced cavalryman's eye, he knew how to inspect dogs for correct conformation and gait. He was, in German shepherd historian Milo Denliger's 1947 description, "an opinionated disciplinarian ... authoritarian, doctrinal and dictatorial ... verein laws were immutable and inflexible. It was typically German, with its hierarchy of authority, which was not to be gainsaid nor questioned." One can imagine the riding crop snapped under the armpit.

In 1923 he published his masterwork, a 700-page tome entitled *The German Shepherd Dog in Word and Picture*, a mix of "valid information and misinformation, outmoded scientific theories, and personal and racial prejudices." It was a book, Denlinger asserts, that "employs Nazism in microcosm long before Nazism was ever heard of under such a name." The book was translated into English and had a profound influence on the development of the dog in the United States, though ultimately the American club would establish its own lines and methodologies.

Von Stephanitz reigned over the German shepherd club until 1935. He resigned, according to one source because of ill health, according to another because Hitler wanted his own people managing the genetics of this most German breed. A year later, on April 22, 1936, von Stephanitz collapsed at his writing desk and died. It was the anniversary day of the founding of the club in 1899. The German national dog championships in Cologne convened a few days later, and competitors and their dogs assembled in the main judging ring for a tribute to von Stephanitz. The speech in his honor ended with the rousing, if ominous, words, "We raise our arms in the German salutation and salute our dead captain!" As Denlinger describes it, after a minute of silence was observed, the climax of the event occurred as the dogs were ordered to "speak," and "Loud and clear their voices sounded over the showgrounds in a last greeting to the creator of the breed."

For all his faults, von Stephanitz did establish the template and bring to fruition the German shepherd dog as a distinctly recognizable breed: intelligent, efficient, protective, hardworking, loyal, and, despite his protestations, even beautiful. Most important of all these attributes, the dogs' temperament and working qualities were coaxed into full bloom. Almost immediately after the breed was formed, von Stephanitz established working trials as part of juried competition, and with the growth of urban centers, he crusaded for police use of the dog--to locate criminals and find lost children or drunks. Though there was initial resistance to the idea, it gradually spread throughout Europe. By the time the idea was up and running, the dogs naturally fell into the role of war dogs. During World War I, the Germans employed some 28,000 dogs, many of them German shepherds. After the war, the first guide dogs, German shepherds, were trained to assist veterans who had been blinded in the war.

Two German shepherds traveled from Germany to the United States at the end of World War I who were to have a major impact on the popularity of the breed in this country. The first was Strongheart, a police dog who was discovered and brought to Hollywood by Larry

Trimble, a producer and animal trainer, and his associate, writer Jane Murfin, and who would become a major movie star. Strongheart's awesome physical appearance and skillful on-camera exploits took America by storm. He was also the subject of the 1954 book *Kinship with All Life*, by J. Allen Boone, which describes not the dog's movie career, but the extraordinary experiences in communication that occurred between Boone and the dog while Strongheart stayed with Boone over a period of many weeks.

Strongheart had the breeding and the training, but it was only after he had connected with Trimble that he evolved into the great working dog for which he became renowned. According to Boone, Strongheart was, "a big, magnificently built dog who did almost incredible things and did them with an intelligence and ease that baffled conventional explanation....He was powerfully built, unusually capable and utterly fearless. His weight fluctuated between 115 and 125 pounds, yet he moved with amazing speed and agility." What liberated the dog from his rote, trained behavior when first acquired, and turned him into a communicative and charismatic actor-dog was his close bond with Trimble, a connection that drew on the talents and graces that were previously "buried beneath the dog's tough physical exterior."

Strongheart paved the way for Rin Tin Tin, who became his box office rival. Rin Tin Tin has outlasted Strongheart in our cultural consciousness because Strongheart made only a handful of films. Strongheart suffered an early death that resulted weeks after a seemingly benign accident on a film set. Rin Tin Tin, however, went on the make forty films in a career that lasted from 1923 until 1932. His dedicated following at the Saturday matinees propped up the floundering Warner Brothers studio, permitting them to remain in existence until they produced *The Jazz Singer,* which gave them new life. Rin Tin Tin stories were, oddly, not considered good material for talkies, or at any rate perhaps the studio was just ready to move onto other things, but his popularity continued for decades in the television series *The Adventures of Rin Tin Tin,* in which his role was played by his descendants, all of whom were trained by his original owner, Lee Duncan.

As a soldier in World War I, Duncan had found a newborn litter of puppies with their mother, a German war dog who had escaped her kennel during an Allied bombing. She had dug a hole, delivered the puppies, and was starving and barely alive when Duncan happened across them during an inspection of the captured site. The camp's other dogs, who had remained in the kennels during the attack, had been killed. The mother and puppies were nursed back to health and distributed among the soldiers of the unit. Duncan took two of the puppies and named them Rin Tin Tin and Nanette after good luck dolls that were commonly given out to troops in France during the war. Duncan lived constantly in the presence of the two dogs and worked with them for hours daily. He had grown up with dogs and had a deep affinity for them. When he was wounded, he arranged to have the dogs stay with him in the hospital, where they entertained others of the wounded with the tricks and exercises taught to them by Duncan, making them in effect the first hospital therapy dogs.

Duncan was able, through a spate of bureaucratic machinations, to bring both dogs back with him when he returned home. Reportedly the more intelligent and skilled of the two dogs, Nanette contracted pneumonia during the voyage to the United States, and died a few weeks after her arrival. Rin Tin Tin lived a long healthy life, and died suddenly, after a play session together, in Duncan's arms, with Hollywood neighbor Jean Harlow beside them.

Rin Tin Tin, for better or worse, inspired several generations of German shepherd dog lovers. Then as now, the quality of a breed declines in direct opposition to its popularity, so with the rage for German shepherds after World War I and again after their legendary bravery in World War II, faults in temperament such as overprotectiveness, over-shyness, and aggression, as well as physical weaknesses such as hip dysplasia found their way into the breed.

Rin Tin Tin himself was not considered show quality by the fancy, and at any rate was ineligible for registration as a purebred since his own parentage was unknown. What Rin Tin Tin demonstrated, though, was that he had all the truly great qualities for which the breed was originally conceived. He was a great working dog, with the abilities and zeal for performance that were originally intended for the breed. He proved that the strict adherence to the decreed standards of conformation need not be what determines the dog's best qualities. Physically, he recalls the head and body type of the earliest official German shepherd dogs, Horand and his progeny. Did Rin Tin Tin's greatness emerge from within his unknown breeding? Or was it the product of the inextricable connection he had formed with Lee Duncan? Had Duncan coaxed this marvelous being from the mass of genetic potential through his intimate bond with the dog? This was surely a case of man-dog spiritual confluence.

The image of Rin Tin Tin, so reminiscent of the early ideal of the dog in both body type and persona, predicts, I believe in a striking way, the sort of dogs that performed as scouts in Vietnam. Some of these dogs were acquired directly from breeders in Germany and the United States; most were donated by families; and few were considered ideal dogs. Whether from breeders or families, the dogs had basically "washed out" from their intended careers, ironically paralleling their handlers. Jesse Mendez explained that they might have been difficult to handle as pets or imperfect as potential material for the show ring. Having failed, in the eyes of the owners, at their prescribed vocations, these dogs became the equivalent to a man categorized as "4-F," eligible for the draft. One dog had been convicted of biting three people and "sentenced to the gas chamber." On appeal, the judge allowed the dog to enter the military instead, where he had a successful career as a scout dog in Vietnam.

Despite their effectiveness in wartime and the truth that they saved thousands of lives, there is still something intrinsically disturbing in the notion of sending dogs to war. They seem excruciatingly vulnerable. That may be a patronizing attitude--the belief that their minds are too simple to manage the pressures and evade the dangers of war. Or it may be a cynical belief that the military won't care properly for the dogs. Evidence points to the contrary in both scenarios. More likely, service in Vietnam gave these particular dogs their second chance, and the life they would lead there-- in the near-constant company of a loving handler who provided them with exciting, active days and nights--

may have compensated for the fear and physical discomforts they underwent, may even have been preferable to the alternatives of euthanasia or eventless, isolated years chained to a dog house, each a sentence to a wasted existence.

To be accepted by the military, the dogs didn't necessarily need to be purebred as long as they were predominantly German shepherd; males were left intact to preserve aggressiveness, while females were spayed to keep them continually fit for service. All dogs were procured through the Lackland Air Force Base, in Lackland, Texas, and then dispersed to the various branches on request for training and use. The dogs were tested for temperament at Lackland and had to pass a physical.

According to John Delware of the training 26th IPSD, "More aggressive dogs were kept as sentry and the less aggressive were sent to us. 'Aggressive' being a word that varied with individual interpretation. Purebred dogs stayed at Lackland and we got the mixed breeds, which were 'more easily trained.'"

While Delware was implying that Lackland may have intended to skim off the cream of the dogs, passing the inferior dogs along to the Army, such a policy may actually have given them better scout dogs. If the Air Force wanted to keep the most aggressive, least friendly dogs for themselves to be used as sentries, while sending dogs of a lesser (that is, less pure) quality to the Army to be trained as scouts, it was a serendipitous arrangement.

More than a few of the dogs that became scouts were said to be crosses with collies or huskies, Labradors or Rottweilers, yet they were still essentially German shepherds. When different dog breeds commingle, all sorts of surprising genetic magic can occur. Possibly, by allowing some freedom in the lines, some of the older, original shepherd dog genes had re-emerged, producing dogs that were closer to the scrappy, adaptive, thinking, flexible, joyful, vivacious, more compact or chunkier, flowing-tailed, straight-backed, personable dogs that populated the early ranks of the German shepherd dog. The looser-lined dogs may well have been better suited to the work of scouting, which often demanded quick, creative thinking. Some may have possessed especially sensitive and receptive minds.

Did that make them better candidates for the sort of communion with humans that would become vital to their survival in Vietnam? The sentry dog handlers also experienced extremely close ties with their dogs. It was typical for a sentry dog (or scout for that matter) to have to be muzzled, or on occasion shot and killed, for medics to attend to his injured handler.

But scouting was another experience altogether. Man and dog were essentially set out into the wilderness to survive. There were no parameters, no finite boundaries of relative safety, as could be said for a sentry and dog guarding a base. The scout dog and handler were cut loose, surrounded from all sides, including above and below, with potential danger. Not only that, there was a line of men behind them depending on the scout and the handler to foresee those dangers. The job didn't begin and end in a pre-ordained segment of hours; it went on for days and nights. And it forged a physical and spiritual closeness between them. Stripped of conventional civilization, the most ancient of inter-species connections took hold.

The dogs did not perform flawlessly, but they were

well suited for the job they were given. As hard-to-handle, overactive dogs, they thrived on the thrill of unknown adventures and unexpected challenges. As, for the most part, extra-intelligent dogs, the busy minds that had gotten them into trouble as housepets now gave them their best chance for survival in the jungles or mountains or paddies and villages.

The Air Force or the Army looked at it more simply. These dogs, as they were assessed for the military, were most likely considered as described by Bert Hubble:

"Sergeant Passmore, a training sergeant, would go around to all the animal shelters and pounds looking for dogs. He always took a tennis ball with him. By bouncing the ball and watching the way the dog reacted, he could tell if the dog was a good prospect for the program. They needed to be fairly aggressive to be scout dogs, but you did not want a really mean dog either. Some dogs proved to be too timid or not trainable to be good working dogs. Sergeant Passmore with his tennis ball tried to select the right ones."

How they reacted to that tennis ball would determine the course of their lives, their passage to Vietnam.

---

Notes

Introductory war dog historical information: Lemish, and interviews with Lemish and Jesse Mendez, former head training sergeant of the Ft. Benning Scout Dog Training School.

As recently as the mid-1980s, the military was discovered to be using dogs unethically when they suspended the animals in nets and used them as targets to test the effects of certain kinds of bullets. When this was made public, a horrified Secretary of Defense, Casper Wineberger (himself a dog lover), terminated the practice immediately.

Though the use of dogs in the Korean war was limited, the major lessons from that experience would be learned again in Vietnam--the preference for small missions of not more than four days' duration; their usefulness in reconnaissance and ambush setups; the need for reward-oriented training refreshers; the effects of wind and terrain conditions; the need for briefing by commanding officers (though there were still problems of officers not accepting handlers' warnings); Asian dislike of dogs; and the importance of the dog-human bond.

Marine report on dogs: p. 129, Lemish.

After World War I, the British changed the name of the dog to "Alsatian wolf-dog," after the French had already rechristened the dog the *chien de Berger Alsace*. The English quickly dropped the wolf-dog portion of the name, fearing the negative image, but held onto he Alsatian tag until 1979.

Description of German shepherd dog: pp. 582-83, *Complete Dog Book.*

Wolves mixed into dog breeding: Lanting, p. 3.

Information on Max von Stephanitz: Denlinger, pp. 24, 26, 27, 55; Palika, p. 18 (on Hitler).

Strongheart: Boone, pp. 13-14, 88.

Rin Tin Tin: English.

The Vietnam war saw a dramatic increase in the use of military dogs--in 1966 scout dog units in training at Ft. Benning, each with more than twenty dog-man teams, soared from one to seventeen; in 1967, more than 2,000 dogs were required by the military, all branches included. Ft. Benning itself purchased 247 German shepherds from Lackland in 1966, 398 in 1967, and requested provisions to purchase 600 for 1968. Actually getting the dogs took time: dogs arrived approximately sixty days after the required forms were filed and then were quarantined for twenty-one days before being brought into the dog population. Unit Historical Activities, 26th IPSD, 1966; History Of Scout Dog Detachment 1967, U.S. Army Information Center, HQ Detachment Scout Dog, U.S. Army, Courtesy U.S. Army Military History Institute.

"Condemned" dog to Vietnam: Bowen, "Canine Scouts," *Leatherneck,* July 1967, p. 26.

While Bert Hubble's story of his sergeant obtaining dogs from local shelters seems to contradict the official procurement policy, he stands by his story. Dogs may have been added in as needed in this way.

---

Captions

p. 211: Bruce Carroll and Fritzie 0X05.

p. 212: Clinton Epps and Fritz 3M75.

p. 213: Richard Hong and Ebony 030M.

p. 214: Duke 96M0.

p. 215: Thunder X229.

p. 217: Little Joe 223M.

p. 220: Bruce Carroll and Fritzie.

# Bibliography

Arluke, Arnold, and Clinton R. Sanders. *Regarding Animals*. Philadelphia, Temple University Press, 1996.

Atkinson, Rick. *The Long Gray Line*. 1989. New York: Henry Holt, 1999.

Bean, Joel. "Scout Dogs Hot on the Enemy's Trail." *Rendezvous With Destiny*. Summer 1970. 10-13.

Bekoff, Marc. *Minding Animals: Awareness, Emotions, and Heart*. New York: Oxford University, 2002.

Bennett, Jane G. *The New Complete German Shepherd Dog*. New York: Howell, 1982.

Berger, John. *About Looking*. New York: Vintage, 1991.

Boone, J. Allen. *Kinship with All Life*. New York: Harper & Row, 1954.

Bowen, Bob, SSgt. "Canine Scouts." *The Leatherneck*. July 1967. 22-27.

Burnam, John. *Dog Tags of Courage*. Ft. Bragg, CA: Lost Coast, 2000.

Campden-Main, Simon M. *A Field Guide to the Snakes of South Vietnam*. Washington, DC: U.S. National Museum, 1970; rep. Lindenhurst, NY: Herpetological Search Service & Exchange, 1984.

Capote, Truman. *A Christmas Memory*. New York: Random House, 1956.

Caputo, Philip. *A Rumor of War*. New York: Henry Holt, 1977; 1996.

Clark, William Henry Harrison, Col. *The History of the United States Army Veterinary Corps in Vietnam, 1962-1973*. Roswell, GA, Wolfe Associates, n.d. (Write: Box 8, Ringgold, GA 30736.)

Coetzee, J.M. *The Lives of Animals*. Princeton: Princeton University Press, 1999.

*The Complete Dog Book*. New York: Howell Book House, 1992; 18th ed.

Conant, Susan. *A New Leash on Death*. New York: Berkley Publishing Group, 1990.

Currey, Richard. *Fatal Light*. New York: Houghton Mifflin, 1988.

Denlinger, Milo G. *The Complete German Shepherd*. New York: Howell, 1947.

Densford, Daniel D. "Thy Scent, Thy Doom." *Rendezvous with Destiny*. Winter 1968-69. 28-31.

Dougan, Clark, and Stephen Weiss. *The American Experience in Vietnam*. New York: W.W. Norton, 1988.

Dyer, Gwynne. *War*. New York: Crown, 1985.

# Bibliography

Ebert, James R. *A Life in a Year: The American Infantryman in Vietnam, 1965-1972*. Novato, CA: Presidio Press, 1995.

English, James W. *The Rin Tin Tin Story*. New York: Dodd, Mead & Co., 1950.

Eighner, Lars. *Travels with Lizbeth*. New York: Fawcett Coumbine, 1993.

*Encyclopedia of American History*. Ed. Richard B. Morris. New York: Harper & Row, 1982.

Farrish, Terry. *Flower Shadow*. New York: William Morrow, 1992.

Fitzgerald, Frances. *Fire in the Lake: The Vietnamese and the Americans in Vietnam*. 1972. New York: Vintage Books, 1989.

Fogle, Bruce. *The Dog's Mind*. New York: Howell Book House, 1990.

Fussell, Paul. *Wartime: Understanding and Behavior in the Second World War*. New York: Oxford University Press, 1989.

Gerstenfeld, Sheldon, V.M.D. *ASPCA Complete Guide to Dogs*. San Francisco: Chronicle, 1999.

Griffin, Donald R. "Animal Consciousness." *Neuroscience & Biobehavioral Reviews*, vol. 9 (1985)., 615-22.

Hearne, Vicki. *Animal Happiness*. New York: HaperCollins, 1994; HaperPerennial, 1995.

Haran, Peter. *Trackers: The Untold Story of the Australian Dogs of War.* Sydney: New Holland Publishers, 2000.

Hedges, Chris. *War is a Force that Gives Us Meaning.* New York: Public Affairs, 2002.

Herr, Michael. *Dispatches.* New York: Avon Books, 1978.

Jamieson, Neil L. *Understanding Vietnam.* Berkeley: U of California Press, 1995.

Jennings, Maj. Paul B., and Moe, Capt. James B. "Veterinary Medicine and Surgery in the Republic of Vietnam." *Military Medicine Journal.* 138:10 (Oct. 73). 633-36.

Karnow, Stanley. *Vietnam: A History.* 1983. New York: Penguin, 1997.

Kieda, Rene. *Fire From Above.* Milford, OH: Riehle Foundation, 1998.

Koehler, William R. *The Koehler Method of Dog Training.* 1962. New York: Howell Book House, 1967.

Knapp, Caroline. *Pack of Two.* New York: Delta, 1998.

Lanting, Fred L. *The Total German Shepherd Dog.* Loveland, CO: Alpine Publications, 1990.

Linzey, Andrew. *Animal Theology.* Urbana and Chicago: U of Illinois Press, 1995.

Lemish, Michael G. *War Dogs: A History of Loyalty and*

# Bibliography

*Heroism.* Washington, D.C.: Batsford Brassey, 1999.

_____ and SFC Jesse Mendez. "Forever Forward: America's Courageous Canine Corps." *Vietnam.* Oct. 1996. 39-44.

Lorenz, Konrad. *Man Meets Dog.* 1953. New York: Kodansha America, 1994.

Martin, Bruce, SSgt. "Scout Dogs." *The Leatherneck.* January 1969. 36-41.

"Medical Care of Vietnam War Dogs." *Journal of the American Veterinary Medical Association.* 156 (1970). 405-08.

Morgan, Paul. B. *K-9 Soldiers: Vietnam and After.* Central Point, OR: Hellgate Press, 1999.

Morris, Desmond. *Dogwatching.* New York: Three Rivers Press, 1986.

Muir, John. *Nature Writings: The Story of My Boyhood and Youth, My First Summer in the Sierra, The Mountains of California, Stickeen, Selected Essays.* New York: The Library of America, 1997.

O'Brien, Tim. *If I Die in a Combat Zone.* New York: Dell, 1969.

_____. *The Things They Carried.* New York: Broadway Books, 1990.

Palika, Liz. *The German Shepherd Dog: An Owner's Guide to a*

*Happy Healthy Pet.* New York: Howell, 1995.

Powell, Mary Reynolds. *A World of Hurt: Between Innocence and Arrogance in Vietnam.* Chesterland, OH: Greenleaf Enterprises, 2000.

*Reporting Vietnam.* New York: The Library of America, 1998.

Scott, John, and John L. Fuller. *Genetics and the Social Behavior of the Dog.* Chicago: U Chicago Press, 1965; 1974.

Seguin, Marilyn W. *Dogs of War: And Stories of Other Beasts of Battle in the Civil War.* Boston: Brandon, 1998.

Serpell, James, ed. *The Domestic Dog: Its Evolution, Behaviour, and Interactions with People.* Cambridge: Cambridge U Press, 1995.

Shay, Jonathan. *Achilles in Vietnam: Combat Trauma and the Undoing of Character.* New York: Simon & Schuster, 1994.

Spector, Ronald H. *After Tet: The Bloodiest Year in Vietnam.* New York: Vintage Books, 1994.

Steinman, Ron. *Women in Vietnam: The Oral History.* New York: TV Books, 2000.

Strickland, Winifred, and James Moses. *The German Shepherd Today.* New and Revised Edition.

Summers, Jr., Harry G. *Vietnam War Almanac.* New York: Facts on File, 1985.

Tripp, Nathaniel. *FatherSoldierSon.* South Royalton, VT:

Steerforth Press, 1998.

Turbak, Gary. "Saluting Canine Courage." *Veterans of Foreign Wars.* February 2000, pp. 12-16.

Wade, Nicholas. "From Wolf to Dog, Yes, but When?" *New York Times,* November 22, 2002. A18.

Wolff, Tobias. *In Pharaoh's Army.* New York: Vintage Books, 1995.


Websites:

Vietnam Dog Handlers Association: www.vdhaonline.org

47th Infantry Platoon Scout Dog: www.47ipsd.us

# Acknowledgments

When I entered into the subject of military dogs and handlers in the Vietnam war, I was writing a monthly column about pets for *Country Living* magazine. Human-animal kinship and communication had fascinated me all of my life, and the topic of men and dogs together at war occurred to me as the most intense relationship of that sort that could possibly exist. I wrote on the subject for an article that appeared in November 1999, but I knew that I had only scratched the surface, and I have remained involved with the subject ever since. In the beginning, I knew something about dogs but little about war. In fact, I admit to a certain trepidation about contacting Vietnam war veterans, given their negative image of earlier years. They were wary of me wishing to write about them for the same reason—would I simply perpetuate those myths?

Seven years ago, I contacted Bert Hubble and Jonathan Wahl, original members of the 47th Infantry Platoon Scout Dog when it came to Vietnam, to ask them if I might write about their time in the war. After careful questioning, they allowed me in, opening the doors for me to their fellow veteran dog handlers. These men have trusted me with their story; many have embraced me as a sister. The timing was right: many had just begun the process of confronting their long-buried memories of the war, their sometimes half-remembered, painful, or fractured histories. I have made every effort to be faithful to the facts and spirit of each experience, and I thank all who shared them with me.

From the 47th IPSD: I am deeply grateful to Rusty

Allen, who lent me his unpublished memoir and checked most of the information I received from others, John Carter, Otis Johnson, Jim Powrzanas, and Larry Proper, principal players in the book, who withstood multiple interviews over the years, as well as Bert Hubble and Jonathan Wahl, Jonathan Harraden, Don Jestes, Stanley Stockdale, Michael Yalango, Joe McMahon, and Steve Lemish, and all the members of the unit, who swapped stories, filled in blanks, shared pictures and videos, and provided fellowship. Handlers from other dog units who helped out include, especially, Randy Kimler, and also Robert Kollar, and in the early stages, Tim Meade, Steve Janke, and Tom Mitchell.

Infantry veterans who offered their own perspective include, most especially John Herschelman, without whom this book would not exist, and Cliff Searcy, and also Curt Knapp, Parker Stockdale, Jeff Cahen, John Delware, A. J. Golden, Mark Orr, and many others who graciously answered my questions over the years.

Special thanks to Sergeant Jesse Mendez and Dr. Howard Hayes for their patience and invaluable contributions, as well as to Michael Lemish, author of *War Dogs: A History of Loyalty and Heroism*, who provided support and friendship, along with invaluable information.

In the writing of the book, I'd like to thank Marjorie Gage and Tom Claire, editors formerly of *Country Living*, for giving me the column and making me a better writer, Colleen Mohyde, for initial guidance, as well as Symmes Gardner, Barbara Kolb of the American Kennel Club library, David Pearce, and Janet Foster of Pacific Gardens Chapel, the last two for helping me search for Marvin Pearce's family. My friends Liza Voges, Maurice Berger, and Marvin Heiferman all generously gave professional advice as well as moral support. Mary Sears, Linda Gentry, John Tessaro, Franc Nunoo-Quarcoo, and Maria Phillips, I thank for steadfast friendship.

To my family, I offer thanks for years of enduring my notions about animals, especially my parents, who first taught them to me, and my brothers, Andy, who gave technical help with maps and more, Lex, and Matthew LaMotte, as well as my nephew Matthew, Jr., and cousin Richard, who read the manuscript and offered advice. Deepest gratitude goes to my mother, who kept the lights on when things got very dim. Finally, I thank Daphne, Marina, and Julian, who both encouraged this effort and absorbed its collateral effects with grace and strength.

Baltimore, May 2006

## About the Author

Toni Gardner has worked as a writer, editor, and photographer for thirty years. A lifelong advocate for animals, she was a contributing editor at *Country Living* magazine, where she wrote the monthly column "You and Your Pet." She wrote *The Complete Dog Book for Kids* (1996) for the American Kennel Club and is a former board member of the Maryland SPCA. She lives in Baltimore, Maryland, with her three children, three dogs, four cats, eight finches, two fish, and hamster.